Hard Air

* * * * * * * * * * * *

Adventures from the Edge of Flying

W. Scott Olsen

University of Nebraska Press | Lincoln and London

© 2008 by the Board of Regents
of the University of Nebraska
All rights reserved
Manufactured in the United States
of America

Set in Minion by Bob Reitz.
Designed by Ashley Muehlbauer.

Library of Congress Cataloging-in-Publication Data
Olsen, W. Scott, 1958–
Hard air : adventures from the edge of flying /
W. Scott Olsen.
p. cm.
ISBN 978-0-8032-1144-5 (paper : alk. paper)
1. Airplanes—Piloting—Anecdotes. 2. Air pilots—
Anecdotes. 3. Extreme environments—Anecdotes.
4. Aeronautics in meteorology—Anecdotes. 5. Search
and rescue operations—Anecdotes.
6. Aeronautics in forest fire control—Anecdotes. I. Title.
TL710.O53 2008 629.132'52—dc22 2007028908

For my family

And thus, also, the realities of nature resume their pride of place. It is not with metal that the pilot is in contact. Contrary to the vulgar illusion, it is thanks to the metal, and by virtue of it, that the pilot rediscovers nature. As I have already said, the machine does not isolate man from the great problems of nature but plunges him more deeply into them.

—Antoine de Saint-Exupéry
Wind, Sand and Stars

Contents

Illustrations

Acknowledgments

Every book has a long list of people behind the author. These people answer questions, provide information, and offer support, a good reader's eye, or the comfort of a place to stay. And every author owes these people profound thanks. *Hard Air* is no exception. I would never have had the chance to ride with the Hurricane Hunters were it not for the patience and hard work of Kathleen Cordner and Stephanie Frankfurt, both of the United States Air Force. Jessica Brady and Joe Pearce, both at Keesler Air Force Base, helped greatly with filling in gaps in my notes. Maj. Chad Gibson, Keesler Air Force Base, helped me find crucial flight information a year after the flight, and helped me make sure I wasn't terribly wrong about some technical information. Pat Valdata, a fine pilot, was an important first reader for many of these chapters, and a great encouragement. Colin Morton and Mary Lee Bragg opened their home to me when I was on my way to the Arctic, and their friendship made that trip a joy. Rick Joubert and Randy Wood at Canada Post opened the first door to the Arctic for me, and without that favor I could not have had the access I had. Randy Eardley and Rose Davis, both of the National Interagency Fire Center, likewise opened doors and answered a thousand questions. And Dan Ehlen, at MeritCare Medical Center in Fargo, North Dakota, offered me a kind of access to that world I could not have imagined. Mike Paulson and Joanna Keen at the Fargo Jet Center suffered through my questions patiently and offered fine answers. Annette Wenda is the kind of copy editor all authors hope for, and to her I owe tremendous thanks. And, finally, thanks to Rob Taylor, my editor at Nebraska, who saw this project through from first idea to last page.

Introduction

✳ ✳ ✳ ✳

The checklist looks easy, and we go through the steps in order. Control wheel lock: remove. Ignition: off. Master switch: on. Fuel-quantity indicators: check. Flaps: down. Master switch: off. Fuel-shutoff valve: on.

Having squeezed myself into the left seat of a Cessna 152 airplane, a two-seater, white with red stripes, N5329B (pronounced "N five three two nine bravo"), I have to pull my legs back up to my chest to fold them out the door and continue the check.

On the right wing: aileron free and secure. Flaps: secure. Wing tie-down: disconnect. Main wheel tire: inflated. Brakes: not leaking.

Mark Malmberg, my flight instructor, six foot two or three and thin, and sixteen years younger than I am, hands me what looks like a shot glass with a small stem in the middle, and I push it into a sump valve for the wing fuel tank. We both look at the blue aviation gas that fills the cup. No water. No sediment. Then, with a foot on the wing strut and another against the nose, I climb to reach the top of the wing and open the fuel tank. Mark hands me another instrument, a long, narrow glass tube with a hollow center and gallon indicators on the side. I put the tube into the gas tank, and when it hits bottom I put my thumb over the open top to seal the liquid in. Eight gallons on that side.

"Perfect," Mark says.

At the nose, we continue. Engine oil level: five quarts. Fuel strainer: another look for water or junk. Alternator belt: check. Air intake: check. Nose wheel and tire: check. Propeller and spinner: check.

"Wait," Mark says. He runs his hand over the end of one propeller blade. Small scuffs arc the end of the blade, and then there is a small bend in the tip. Mark looks at the other blade. It's clean and straight. "We need someone to look at this," Mark says.

Even though it's lunch hour, a mechanic comes out, as does one of the other flight instructors. No instructor has flown this plane for more than a week. It's all been private rentals. Still, the mechanic says, looking at the good blade, it doesn't look like it was hit while spinning. Mark mentions that the scuffs are the same color as the equipment the line men use to move planes around. Maybe someone just ran into it, he suggests.

"Are you going to say it's okay to fly?" Mark asks.

"I'm not making *that* call," says the mechanic.

Then the chief mechanic comes out. He runs his hand over the bend. He agrees that the bend looks like a hit from a line truck. "Sorry," he says. "We should fix this before you fly."

We reconnect the tie-downs, and close the doors.

"Sorry," Mark says.

It's a beautiful day for flying. Overhead, bright sun and little wind. Small cotton-ball clouds. Other private planes take off and land in front of us. We don't even get the engine started. That bend could shake the engine right out of the plane. But already, I think, I've learned something. I saw that bend and those scuffs. Nearly everything I own has similar evidence of age and use and effort. I would have thought, and did think, nothing of it.

* * *

For as long as I can remember, I have been watching airplanes. Craning my neck when they have been far overhead, pausing near airports to watch them take off or land, reading about them in waiting-room magazines and books, stopping to scan the sky when my ears have recognized the sound of a prop working the air, I have wondered what it would be like to fly. There have been moon-filled nights on the highways when I've felt the miles under each tire and I've pulled back just slightly on the steering wheel, imagining the easy lift, the nose of my Jeep tilting toward the sky, smiling at the silly hope.

On my computer, I've flown everywhere from Kitty Hawk to the Gamma Quadrant. I've flown everything from a balloon to the SR-71. I can talk about wing loading, weight and balance, STOL kits, scramjets. I can talk about missions, too. Helicopter rescues in oceans or jungles, reconnaissance missions in storms, research above seventy thousand feet. And I can sound like I know what I'm saying. But in truth, I know almost nothing. What I know, I know from books. What I know lacks any kind of experience, any kind of truth that matters.

I know the planes and the helicopters are there. I've seen the pictures and read the articles. I know what they do. But I do not know the feel of the thing in my hands and under my feet. I know what the missions are, but I have no idea what they are like. And I am curious—deeply, ferociously curious. So I am learning to fly. And I am tagging along.

This is a book about extraordinary flying. But this is not a book about fighter pilots or astronauts, the easy stories of fast drama, hero making, or tragedy. This is book about the more ordinary flying, in conditions that would keep fighters locked on the carrier deck and rockets glued to the launchpad. What crawled under my imagination when I was very young were the stories about flying in places no one should be flying. Hurricanes. Firestorms. Deep engine-killing cold. What crawled under my imagination, and stayed there, were the stories about rescue missions, or the long, lonely flights just for information to keep other people safe.

What is it like to fly this way, I wondered? Who are these people?

* * *

Running errands all day. I drop off a roll of film to be developed and turn my Jeep toward the airport. I need the computer disks for the ground school and my own headset for the airplane. And I swear this is the truth—too good to be made up. The minute I turn the Jeep toward the airport, National Public Radio brings me a rendition of *Also Sprach Zarathustra*. The theme from *2001: A Space Odyssey*.

I am about to get the computer disks to help me fly, and behind the dramatic music I hear the frighteningly calm voice of Hal: "I'm sorry, Dave. I can't do that."

* * *

Mark and I, finally flying, are going through the early basics. Climbing turns. Descending turns. Flying straight and level. We put the flaps down, pull the engine power back to idle, and practice best glide speed. We talk about how to avoid the geese that appear over the runway just before takeoff.

It's another soft and bright summer day. I watch cars on gravel roads lift plumes of dust, and then watch those plumes move across fields. I watch the way sunlight glints off river water and ponds. I watch kids on soccer fields, and, amazed, at four thousand feet I watch a red-tailed hawk soar another thousand feet above me. The plane is easy in my hands.

"See?" Marks says, teasing. "Nothing to it!"

Suddenly, the radio gets interesting.

"I may have to switch over to emergency," a voice says calmly.

Mark and I grow quiet and look at each other.

"I can see the highway patrol," the voice says.

"It's not the plane," Marks tells me.

We listen as the pilot leads police to some truck speeding away. But when we land, no one at the flight school has heard the radio traffic.

The next morning's newspaper tells the story of a crop duster assaulted by his drunken boss at the airfield. The pilot took off and then called the police. The boss drove away, and the pilot followed him in the plane. When the police showed up, the pilot directed them from the air.

* * *

Bad weather descends onto this part of the Dakota border, and most planes are grounded. Forty-knot winds press the windows of my house, and fat rain screams by horizontal to the ground. Across town, however, the commercial jets are still flying.

At home, I am in a large chair and hold the books and the journals, the voices that seem to echo the sky.

> The price of their ambition is a life closer to death; they suffer more heart attacks and aneurysms and ruptures than any other living creature. It's expensive to fly. You burn out. You fry the machine. You melt the engine. Every creature on earth has approximately two billion heartbeats to spend in a lifetime. You can spend them slowly, like a tortoise, and live to be two hundred years old, or you can spend them fast, like a hummingbird, and live to be two years old.
> —Brian Doyle, "Joyas Voladoras"

I am only an amateur, and I shouldn't be talking.

But I can't help talking. You take the air: the thin, substance-less air that can be made to bear a man; you take America; and you take an airplane, which of all the works of man is the nearest to a living being—you take those things and mix them up, and they will act as a drug which will knock all proper reticence right out of you.

And so, here I go talking.

—Wolfgang Langewiesche, *America from the Air*

Tom taught me in a D. H. Gipsy Moth, at first, and her propeller beat the sunrise silence of the Athi Plains to shreds and scraps. We swung over the hills and over the town and back again, and I saw how a man can be a master of a craft, and how a craft can be master of an element. I saw the alchemy of perspective reduce my world, and all my other life, to grains in a cup. I learned to watch, to put my trust in other hands than mine. And I learned to wander. I learned what every dreaming child needs to know—that no horizon is so far that you cannot get above it or beyond it. These I learned at once. But most things came harder.

—Beryl Markham, *West with the Night*

Morning after morning, a flyer sat here and felt of a sudden, somewhere inside the vulnerable man subjected to his neighbor's surliness, the stirring of the pilot of the Spanish and African mails, the birth of him who, three hours later, was to confront in the lightnings the dragon of the mountains; and who, four hours afterwards, having vanquished it, would be free to decide between a detour over the sea and a direct assault on the Alcoy range, would be free to deal with storm, with mountain, with ocean.

—Antoine de Saint-Exupéry, *Wind, Sand and Stars*

What is the hope or the need that compels us into the air? Why do I have this desire to fly? Why do small children make paper airplanes, and why do adults take lessons when they have no wish to become commercial pilots?

There is still, I think, in most of us, the urge to explore.

* * *

Hector International Airport, in Fargo, North Dakota, is home to Mark and the 152, any number of private airplanes of all sorts, the Fargo Flight School, a company called Weather Modification—one of the last serious cloud-seeding operations that works all over the world—an avionics company and maintenance company, a commercial terminal for Northwest and United and sometimes others, and also the F-16s of the 119th Fighter Wing, the North Dakota Air Guard, the Happy Hooligans. It can get to be a busy place.

A clear-sky afternoon, and Mark is helping me smooth out my landings. We're in the pattern, which only means we're flying a rectangle around the airport and each time coming in for a touch-and-go landing. My brain knows how to land. I can recite the rules. But it takes some time to get the feel of the dance. Aim for the runway numbers. Watch airspeed. Learn by sight where to level off and when to flare.

We turn from the base leg of the approach to final, a long final approach for us as we had to wait for some departing traffic, and I'm getting set up when suddenly the tower clears three F-16s to cut in front of us and land. Literally dropping out of the sky from well above us, the jets loop into the pattern like curveballs thrown from Olympus.

Mark can hardly stay in the airplane. "Wow! Look at that!" His excitement is huge in the plane. I almost ask him if he'd like to help me peddle faster to catch up. "I've got to remember to bring my camera!" he exclaims. "I mean, you'll never see that again!"

Mark strains against the seat belt to watch each jet arc into view and then land. We are in slow flight, an airspeed of fifty-five knots into a headwind that makes our ground speed a fair bit slower. The tower clears a military tanker to take off in front of us, and then the tower gives us an advisory for wake turbulence.

No kidding, I think.

* * *

First solo—day one. Rain.

First solo—day two. Thirty-knot wind.

First solo—day three. Rain.

First solo—day four. Alternator out on the 152.

First solo—day five. Clear sky, only an eight-knot wind. But it's a crosswind. The school does not allow crosswind landings of more than a few knots for first solos, and does not allow first solos on the short runway that would turn the crosswind into a headwind.

At home, frustrated and anxious, I sip coffee on the back porch with my dog and scan the sky. I watch a commercial jet approach for a landing. I hear a crop duster in the distance. And I smile when we are visited by swallows. Common barn swallows, small, V tails and black backs, they do not live in my backyard, nor do they nest under any eave or cornice at my house. Perhaps they live at the Lutheran church next door, or farther away. Maybe they even rest in a barn. I don't really know. I've never followed them home.

But on summer days, when I go into my backyard to cut the grass or run with Chaucer, our collie, a swallow almost always appears, a streak very low to the ground that I catch out of the corner of my eye. Then two. Then perhaps a dozen. They dive and whirl and turn and dart and rise and bank and circle around us. Our movement through the grass raises small white bugs, and the swallows pick them clean out of the air.

And I am convinced there is more to these afternoons than birds feeding. There is something about the way the swallows fly. Something more than instinct or utility.

I have never heard an ornithologist say this, but I am convinced that swallows *play*. I am convinced that swallows fly in part to eat, but also in part for the simple joy of flying. Too many passes go by without food for the swoops to be efficient.

Too many turns turn into rolls that then rise toward the sun for there not to be any small grins in the birds' beaks, or winks in their eyes.

Many times I have stood in my own backyard and watched the swallows. When I pause, Chaucer usually sits by my side and watches with me. And I am tempted to say I am jealous, or perhaps just envious, of the swallows' flight. The ease of it all. The kinetic power and grace and speed. But jealousy and envy do not describe how I feel. If birds play—if birds understand any small bit of the ideas we call beauty, grace, art, or even just fun—then what I feel, honestly, is blessed to stand in the middle of it and be a witness.

Soon, I think.

* * *

First solo comes, and I am surprised by the lack of apprehension. Mark and I fly around the airport a few times to make sure I'm having a good day, and then we pull up to the Jet Center and he gets out. His last act is to call the tower and let them know a student pilot is heading out for a first solo. Then he closes the door, smiles at me, and walks off.

I radio ground control, taxi to the end of the runway, go through the checklists, radio the tower, and am cleared to take off. The 152, lighter now by one person, leaps easily off the runway, and I can feel the smile on my face.

The tower tells me to turn left, which I do, and I meet my first challenge. I am, immediately, going to shred a flock of geese. Birdstrike can bring down a plane this size fast. I pull back on the wheel. The plane climbs, and it's once around the airport for a touch-and-go landing. Three times around the airport, each landing softer and more graceful than the last, and I'm pulling up to the Jet Center again. Mark comes out with another instructor for congratulations and pictures. Turns out they were listening to the scanner and watching the pattern.

"Nervous?" I ask.

"Nah," he says. "We do that for all first solos."

This is, of course, just the beginning. The lessons continue, sometimes with Mark in the plane, sometimes by myself. But each time in the air is a joy. One day, after practice following radio navigation beacons for cross-country flights, we land and are told to hold short on a taxiway while the Hooligans pass on the way to their own hangar. The pilot of the lead jet waves at us and snaps a small salute.

"That was nice," I say, surprised that the pilot of an F-16 would salute a Cessna 152.

"Every single one of them," Marks tell me, "once sat right where you are now."

* * *

I fly a very small airplane. Just two seats. It's loud and it's old, and it is very, very slow. It does not go very high. And this is a choice. I would like to believe there is still some room for adventure. When I am in the air, I want to feel the air. I want to see the earth, the rivers and trees and farmsteads and highways and fence lines and shelterbelts, from a new perspective, and smile when my ideas of home and place are shifted by the larger view. There is a great lesson every time the plane takes off, and I can see how close we all are.

In front of me is still that desire to know what it feels like to be a pilot in hard air. To be a pilot whose flight planning can go only so far before the maps and the rules run out, and then it's just experience and hope and sky. I have the e-mails and letters and questions in front of me. Hurricane Hunters, who fly in the planet's largest storms. The Ice Patrol, airplane heirs of the *Titanic*, searching thousands of square miles of ocean, trying to find the icebergs that could bring down ships. Helicopters that race emergency patients from accident sites or small clinics to larger care. Pilots who land huge and heavy planes on skis and ice, in Greenland and Antarctica. Pilots who carry water and slurry up canyons filled with the smoke of wildfire to dump their loads suddenly and put out the fire. These are the people I want to know. These are the missions I want to feel.

Some pilots would say that real flying is speed and altitude. But there are a whole lot of us who search for the small, the remote, the edge-of-the-map places on the ground or in the sky. What makes these places interesting is the way you have to get there. The flying is simply more challenging, more exciting, more present. The first approach to a new airstrip is a rush of concentration and intimacy, the whole of your body expanded to include the flaps and ailerons, your sense of touch reaching for winds and then the ground. The first pass over ground you've never seen is to feel in your gut the thrill that comes before the celebrated photograph. The long flight to find storm or ice is the hope that what you will find will somehow matter, will save someone's life.

So this is a book about extraordinary flying, about a particular kind of exploration, adventure, and risk. And this is a book about the stories these people tell. Their missions are simple. Get there, be there, get out—alive.

Hard Air

1. The Air in Resolute

✳ ✳ ✳ ✳

Before some adventures, you stare at the maps. There is a long dreamtime first. You find yourself listening to stories, some more closely than others. And what fills the quiet moments is a kind of wondering, the kind of wondering that turns into hope, and then the kind of hope that turns into ambition. That ambition turns into resolve, which turns into planning, and then suddenly it seems, although it's been years coming, you find yourself standing on the edge of something strange and original. Half scared. Half so very much at home you wonder if you can ever go back.

This morning I am on First Air flight 860, a white Boeing 737 with the old torpedo-shaped engines. A Canadian flag is painted just behind the cockpit window. On the tail, an Inukshuk, flat stones stacked into a human shape with arms outstretched, rests on ground before a brilliant blue sky. We are leaving Ottawa and heading toward Iqaluit, the capital of Nunavut, on Baffin Island, Canada. 1,298 miles north. Latitude: 63°45′36″ N. Longitude: 68°33′00″ W. And while the weather this morning in Ottawa is partly cloudy and warm, according to the forecast it's 2°C in Iqaluit now, and snowing. It's the second of June. And after Iqaluit, I am going still a good bit farther north.

We push back from the gate, and the flight attendants act out the safety procedures while recordings in English, French, and Inuktitut play one after the other through the speakers. Then, with the familiar roar and rush of the engines, the jet is in the sky and we are on our way. The captain turns off the seat-belt sign, and the flight attendants come through the cabin and hand out newspapers, the *Ottawa Citizen and Global Mail*, as well as the trilingual *Nunatsiaq News*. Headlines of politics and scandal and local people trying to do well.

But I cannot escape the view outside the window. The landscape of Ontario and then Quebec is rich in green forest and lakes and rivers, beautiful, really, from the air, as my eye tries to play connect-the-lakes-with-the-rivers. Roads dwindle and then disappear entirely. The land becomes rocky, changes from green to brown. Taller hills begin to emerge between the lakes and streams. It's nearly impossible to imagine the Hudson Bay Company or the Native peoples thousands of years before them finding their way in this land, the struggle from point A to B, or the hope in simply setting out from A, when B has not been discovered. Yet one of the early-learned joys of flying is how even the smallest bit of altitude changes forever the pilot's perception of distance. It takes no time at all, and on a clear, fine day not even very much effort or thought, to fly over some hills or a dozen lakes and streams. The world is always as big as our capacity to imagine it, and flying makes it easy to imagine a whole lot more.

However, the plane this morning is heading north, where I will catch another small plane, which will head even farther north. We will cross the Arctic Circle, and keep going. Iqaluit to Igloolik, Igloolik to Pond Inlet, Pond Inlet to Resolute Bay, and then Resolute to Grise Fiord, the northernmost town in Canada. Deep Arctic. Land and sky beyond anything I've seen, and beyond my talent to imagine with any real depth. I've heard stories about the pilots who fly up there, whose off-strip landings are more frequent than on-strip, who land on skis and ice and snow, who fly the plane that seems to be capable of anything—the De Havilland Twin Otter—and I want to meet these people. How do you fly, when the weather is fast and the ground is unsure? How thick does the ice need to be to hold the weight of a landing airplane, and how do you tell before you land? How do you prepare when the satellite telephone rings and someone needs to be rescued from the ice?

There is romance to the idea of flying. There is thrill and danger and skill, and there is supernatural luck as well. But give the flying a purpose, an altruistic purpose, and you have the stuff of legend. Staring at the large map on the wall of my office one day, my eye tracing the outlines of islands named Baffin, Ellesmere, Banks, Devon, Cornwallis, Victoria, Prince of Wales, Somerset, Bathurst, Melville, Bylot, and King William, the names all imposed during a time, for good and evil, of exploration and discovery, I found myself thinking about the people, the Inuit and the European, and what it must be like to live there. And then the obvious came clear to me. These people need supplies. These people get mail! And in the Arctic, mail means airmail.

From the very beginning, the idea of a small plane coming down from the sky with letters and packages and news of the faraway captured something essential in the human spirit. Early pilots, in the open-cockpit days, did not in general live to see their fifth anniversary of service. The weather would turn, and the instruments were poor. It was easy to get lost, to get upside down, to have something break. But delivering the mail had the kind of nobility that made it all worthwhile if not completely necessary.

Where is farthest away, I wondered? How far does the airmail go? Who are the pilots who bring the mail, and what do they face in the sky and on the ground? Some time on the Web gave me a list of air stages for Canada Post. The northernmost delivery site, I learned, is Eureka, on Ellesmere Island. But Eureka is not really a town. It's a civilian weather station, and mail delivery is irregular. More north of Eureka is a place called Alert, but it's a military base and closed to civilians. So the northernmost site of mail delivery is Grise Fiord, population somewhere between 104 and 140, 720 miles north of the Arctic Circle, on the southern end of Ellesmere Island. Latitude: 76°25′00″ N. Longitude: 82°54′0″ W. I had to get there.

When I called Canada Post, it took only two connections before I was talking with a man named Rick Joubert, director of Canada Post's National Control Centre. I told him what I wanted to do.

"We don't go there," he said.

There was a pause in the conversation.

"As a matter of fact, *we* don't fly anywhere," he said. "We contract for that service."

"Is there anyone . . . ," I began.

"The company up there is Kenn Borek," he continued. "Let me call them for you."

* * *

Waiting at a gate window in Ottawa, watching planes take off and land, I spent some time talking with an Air Canada pilot, asking about flying in the Arctic. I could not imagine, I told him, an Arctic filled with the little white omni radio stations that fill the more southern airspace with navigational aids. There's simply too much space in the Arctic. There's not very much in that space, and the environment is hard. GPS, the global positioning system, is effective and easy, and nearly every plane has it. But pilots use the other stuff too. He smiled and said he didn't know much about flying that far north. He'd never been there. Then I mentioned that I'd be riding with the guys from Kenn Borek, and his eyes grew wide. He leaned back and put two thumbs up.

"Oh, those guys! They are legends in the aviation business," this captain said, "and I suppose everything these days is pretty safe. But back then, back when they started, it was whatever looked good."

Back in the First Air flight, I watch the clouds come in, and then I cannot see a thing. The captain turns on the seat-belt sign as we fly through some bumps that would not upset a cup of coffee, and when the clouds part for a moment I see snow and ice hugging the shorelines of lakes, white ribbons marking the boundaries between blue water and brown earth. We begin our descent, and the captain tells us that in Iqaluit the winds are blowing at 45 kilometers per hour out of the north. It's 2°C, and there is rain in the air.

The approach comes in from the east over Frobisher Bay, named for the English sea captain who believed, wrongly, that this bay was the start of the Northwest Passage. The bay is filled with broken ice. After landing and a short taxi we park at the terminal and exit through the rear of the airplane and down stairs. For some reason, the stairs make me happy. I've never liked jetways, the telescoping hallways at nearly every airplane gate, because they remove the whole sense of getting in a machine, of leaving a building and going into something entirely else. With a jetway you go from one bad waiting room to another bad waiting room, which just happens to move. But without one, you have to go outside before you can leave. You have to be in the weather. And you can see the airplane. Not just the nose of it tucked up against a terminal. You see the whole thing, and your eye can send that picture to your brain. You are about to go flying. In this particular machine. In this particular weather. On this particular day.

Outside the airplane, I nearly laugh out loud when I see the terminal. Bright yellow steel, curved at the edges, it looks more like it belongs on the bottom of the sea, tended by a Cousteau or two, than at a Canadian airport. Inside there's a press of people—Inuit, European, Asian—all waiting to board some outbound flight. There are display cases of Inuit artifacts, information boards for the park system, advertising for local hotels. There's even a sign for Subway Sub Shops, reminding me to

Eat Fresh. First Air, Canadian North, and Kenn Borek share the ticket counter.

Getting access to pilots is not an easy task sometimes, and it takes good people to open doors and set a tone. Rick Joubert of Canada Post called Steve Penikett, the general manager of Kenn Borek, who e-mailed Joan Griffin, Borek's general manager of Nunavut Operations in Iqaluit. Joan is the person who makes it all happen. A short woman with a bright smile and an easy laugh, she comes into the terminal waiting area and shakes my hand heartily, and I damn near give her a hug for no good reason. Gracious and hospitable, and no-nonsense too, she hands me the tickets for the next few legs of the trip. Joan has set up these flights for me and told the pilots and the station managers I'm coming. I try to buy her a cup of coffee, eager to hear whatever stories she might hold, but she's too busy, so we agree I'll buy her one on the way back out.

On the terminal television monitors, one for departures and one for arrivals, there is narrative as well as schedules and times. The First Air flight to Clyde River, about halfway up the eastern shore of Baffin Island, I learn, is going to fly directly to Pond Inlet, near the top of the island first, then try Clyde River on return. Right now in Clyde River the weather is bad, and airplanes are not going in or out. This far north, the weather changes fast, and every flight might be a trip to someplace else. My flight to Resolute, however, seems to be doing just fine. No delays. We are scheduled to leave at 2:00. Two stops, one at Igloolik and one at Pond Inlet, before we get to Resolute.

* * *

A Beechcraft 100 is a twin turboprop airplane with a range of nearly 2,000 miles. It can fly above 25,000 feet and has been used for everything from an ambulance to Air Force One. The Beech 100 sitting at the Iqaluit airport this morning, white with thin red and black stripes running the length of the fuselage and then up the tail, tail number C-GHOC, has a luggage pod attached to the underside. The half dozen or so of us passengers exit the terminal and walk to the back of the plane, where the pilots greet us and stand by the stairs. I crawl into the left seat just behind the pilot's. A few minutes later, the two pilots join us, and I'm not sure if I should interrupt, so I simply settle in to watch the preflight checks.

It all seems pretty normal, with one exception. There is a light on the annunciater panel that says the luggage-pod door is open. The pilot points this out to his partner.

"It's definitely closed," the copilot says. "I was just out there. There's just so much pressure against the door, the switch must think it's open. That's been an issue with this airplane. But it's closed."

The pilot nods, and they finish their checks. When they set the altimeter to 29.43, the current local atmospheric pressure, I see the runway is a whole 100 feet above sea level. The copilot turns and smiles, talks to the passengers, goes over the flight time and safely procedures, and then at ten minutes before three, we head toward runway two-five in Iqaluit. At the end of the runway it's power levers forward, and at about 100 knots we rotate and head for the sky.

We climb. The sky above us is a brilliant and clear deep blue. But when we reach 19,800 feet, the clouds below us have thickened, and it's just sheer, smooth white as far as every horizon. With the thrum of the engines in the background, each of us in the passenger seats settles into our own private trance.

"Are you the one who's writing an article?" the copilot asks.

I lean forward and confess, and then it's introductions and handshakes all around. Mario Noel is the pilot. Ron Miller is flying as copilot. Both men look to be in their early to midthirties.

"You're flying with two captains today," Ron tells me. "Mario's new to the company. Not new to the airplane or anything, just new to the company. So this is a kind of orientation."

"Congratulations," I tell him, and Mario gives me a big smile over his shoulder. We try to talk, but the engine noise and the demands of the cockpit make it difficult, and we agree to talk at the first landing. Ron reaches into his backpack, pulls out a sack lunch—a water bottle and sandwich.

When the clouds diminish, I can see below us clear ocean water as well as large floes of ice. Sea ice breaking up. Stress fractures and leads in the ice that remains. Different shades of white turning to blue and the sun reflecting off the water. Clouds casting shadows down onto the water.

It is a beautiful and humbling sight. But one thing remains. Every pilot knows an engine could fail at any moment, for any reason. The Beech could limp along with just one engine, but out here, looking at the ocean, the ice floes, clouds, the sun still high in the sky that will not set for days with me now, what I know is that if an engine were to fail or there were any emergency, we'd be in some serious trouble. Yes, I tell myself, this is a scheduled flight, hauling airmail, cargo, and people to the ends of the earth. There are flight plans and alternate landing sites. But nonetheless, between here and there, we're about as far away from help as people can get.

* * *

At landing, the winds in Igloolik are 210 at 20 knots. In other words, the winds are from the southwest, and blowing about 23 miles an hour. The runway is 149–329 (in other words, it heads northwest and southeast), so there is a bit of a crosswind, but nothing out of the ordinary. The day has become clear and sunny, and I find myself staring at the frozen and snow-covered water of Foxe Basin. According to my map, Igloolik actually sits on a small island. But jump over not very much distance, and I'd be on mainland Canada. In theory, I could walk home from here.

C-GHOC makes a slow descent, and as the plane turns I see

over Ron's shoulder and out the front glass a brown smudge on the snowscape evolve into a straight gravel runway. At the end of the runway, a short drop-off and then the ice of Foxe Basin. But this one is not a problem. Mario nails the landing, and I can barely feel the tires on the gravel. We taxi to the blue terminal building, Ron opens the door, and everyone gets off the plane. Ron and Mario begin to unload baggage from the back and from the pod underneath the airplane, and so I wander into the terminal. A modern ticket counter fronts one wall, while a baggage carousel hugs the other. I look out the front windows and see an Inukshuk framed by a white sign on posts. Welcome to Iglulik. Three snowmobiles are lined up in front of the sign. In the distance and down a hill, the town itself.

A poster in the terminal tells me there's evidence of habitation here for a thousand years—Dorset and Thule cultures. Captains Perry and Lyon of the British Royal Navy were here in 1822. From another poster I learn that the people who live here, the Igloolingmiut, are "fiercely independent and protective of their language and culture. They drew international attention when they rejected television in the '70s until they were satisfied the language and culture would not be threatened." A third poster offers the nutritional value of arctic char, caribou, Perry caribou, polar bear, ringed seal, walrus, narwhal, bowhead whale, beluga, and musk ox.

And it is tempting to simply walk out of this terminal and down the hill. It is hard not to hear the whisper of so many stories and so many histories so very close. To sit down here, and listen, would be one way to know a world I have seen only surfaces of in magazines and other books. But I also know this truth—in every place on the planet, once a person is settled, he or she looks up to the sky and wonders.

The fuel truck arrives, the plane is fueled, a smaller number of us get back on, and Ron closes the door. During the preflight checks he shows me a chart. Iqaluit to Igloolik is 461 miles. It's another 213 to Pond Inlet, and then another 310 to Resolute—984 miles altogether. Not a bad day's flying. But Mario and Ron want to get back in the air as fast as possible. At the moment, the weather in Resolute is fine. But it's closing in at Pond Inlet, where the approach is nonprecision although IFR, or "instrument flight rules." We have to break out of whatever clouds are present at or above 500 feet above ground level, or we cannot land. (In a precision approach, guided by more instruments, we can descend to 200 feet before we leave the clouds. Resolute is a precision approach.) We have enough fuel to reach an alternate airport if Pond Inlet is weathered in, but that does not mean the alternate airport is close, or that the weather there will remain clear.

Mario pushes the power levers forward, and once again we are in the sky, the overcast filling in the view sooner than I hope.

∗ ∗ ∗

There is a story on a Web site for the New York Air National Guard, the group that flies the support missions to the South Pole and trains in Greenland during the summer, of a veteran commercial pilot who was ferrying a small plane across Greenland and tried to descend through a layer of clouds. But what he thought were clouds turned out to be the Greenland ice cap. He survived the crash and waited three days for rescue.

There are a hundred reasons this should not happen. There are instruments and planning and plain good sense. But there is also what pilots call situational awareness. If you lose this, you can usually start chiseling the headstone.

This story comes to mind as we near Pond Inlet and I am watching the top of the cloud layer go by under the airplane. Then a lead, a break in the sea ice, goes by as well. A long, narrow opening in the ice, it stretches from horizon to horizon, and suddenly I have depth perception and contrast back. What I thought were clouds was really the hard, frozen water of Eclipse Sound.

Looking up, I see that Ron and Mario do not have my problem. We continue to lose altitude, right on target, but we are also getting close to the VFR, or visual flight rules, limits. The sky is overcast, the ceiling is low, and it's snowing. And there are mountains here, too. Finally we come below the clouds, fly over the airport, make a bank to the left, come in and level off and flare, and then again the sounds of landing on gravel.

We taxi to the terminal, and, looking out the window, I see the brightly colored homes with steeply pitched roofs. Satellite dishes point nearly horizontal to the ground, aiming for some orbiting dot above the equator. But I cannot see more than half a mile or so into the distance.

"It's too bad the weather is like this," Ron says. "It really is a beautiful place."

Mario and Ron exit the plane with the passengers. "Twenty minutes, tops," Ron says. I decide to huddle back in my seat and close my eyes. We're already a long way from Ottawa. Then Mario reappears. "Looking for a bag!" he says. He digs in the baggage stored in the back, then looks in the pod again, then comes to look once more in the back. "Ah!" he cries, holding up the package, then leaves for the terminal.

The twenty minutes go by. Then another twenty. Snow falls lightly, and the inside of the plane gets cold. Then the two pilots appear, but no passengers are behind them. They crawl into the seats next to me and pull out their charts.

"The weather is Resolute is okay right now," Ron says. "But this place is closing in fast. If we get up in the air, and we can't land at Resolute, I doubt we will be able to return here either."

"We need an alternate in our fuel range," Mario adds.

"I have no doubt we'll land in Resolute," Ron continues. "But we need to have a plan just in case."

There are very few places up here where you can land a plane like this, and so the charts are spread over our laps, and the two men weigh the various options. Mario hasn't been up here before today, so he listens as Ron details the options. But then Mario does have a question.

"You and your bags," he says to me. "A little more than two hundred pounds?"

"Yes," I say.

He turns to Ron. "If we leave him behind, we can fly almost anywhere."

Ron looks at me and smiles. "Resolute is a precision approach. It shouldn't be a problem."

* * *

The approach to Resolute is a beautiful approach. It really is. Glistening ocean ice. Hills rising out of the water into cliffs. Snow on top of the hills. You can see the town around a bend in the island about 10 kilometers from the airport.

We line up with the runway a fair distance out, over a beacon, and on final we come through a light cloud at about 1,000 feet. Ice instantly coats and clings to the front windshields. There's no way to see. The pilots simply look and grin at each other. I do know that descending into warmer air (and sometimes climbing) will remove ice from a plane pretty quick, and I can already see where the windshield heaters are at work, but I wonder if any of the passengers are worried, so I turn and look. Everyone is looking out the side windows. (I later asked Mario if icing on final approach made him nervous. He said, "No, nervous is when that happens and you hit power and the plane won't go back up.")

After we touch down and taxi to the terminal, a man named Ranjit Sangra comes out to the plane and begins to gather the bags. I know the Narwhal Hotel, where I am staying, is at the airport. But I cannot see it.

"Can you point me toward the Narwhal?" I ask.

"Are you Scott?" he asks.

"Yes."

"Rhonda's waiting for you inside."

Rhonda, I discover, is the manager of the Narwhal Hotel. She's here to carry me and my bag to the hotel, as she does for each arriving guest, even though the distance is less than half a mile. She is sitting with Dan Minsky, the station manager for Kenn Borek Air, in an office behind the ticket counter, listening to an ancient high-frequency (HF) radio and smoking cigarettes. Dan, I think, cannot yet be thirty-five years old. He wears a sweatshirt and a baseball cap, and glasses. We all introduce ourselves, and Dan tells me that tomorrow's flight to Grise Fiord has been postponed until four or five o'clock in the evening.

"We've got a bit of a rescue going on up near the North Pole," he says. "When the pilots get back, I need to give them some time to rest."

"Rescue?" I ask. It's clear his real attention is on the radio behind him.

"You can tell him all about that tomorrow," Rhonda says, ushering me out the door. It's ten thirty at night, we're a good bit late, and she's anxious to call it quits. Dan and I promise to meet tomorrow. Rhonda drives me over to the hotel, where she has a dinner wrapped in tinfoil waiting for me. At the Narwhal, you eat whatever the cook decides to cook, and dinner ends at six. This is a good many hours after that, but under the foil I discover a steak, baked potato, garlic shrimp, vegetables. Once heated in the microwave and carried to my room, it is a fine way to end the day. But looking out my window, I see two Twin Otters, painted Kenn Borek colors, red and white with a black lightning bolt down the side, parked side by side, skis attached to the wheels. And I want nothing more than to get inside.

* * *

Saturday morning in Resolute, ten o'clock, and the skies are overcast and gray. Snow is falling, enough of it to dust the ground. Visibility from the front step of the Narwhal is a bit more than a mile, and the winds are light. Both Twin Otters are already gone.

Inside the hotel, airplane pilots, helicopter pilots, mechanics, and others watch TV, play pool, sit in the dining room and talk. The cook, a man in a double-breasted white chef's jacket and crisp black pants, has just finished serving a large breakfast— three or four different kinds of eggs, bacon, sausage, potatoes, and more. The coffee is good and strong. Everyone now seems to be waiting for the weather, or for the next assignment.

The walk from the hotel to the terminal and the Kenn Borek office passes a blue building, the main base for the Polar Continental Shelf Project, a part of the Canadian government that provides ground and air support for researchers in the Arctic. They contract with the Kenn Borek pilots and planes for the air work. After the blue building there is an open and snow-covered plain on the right, dipping down toward the sea, and the hangars and workshops and offices of the airport on the left. All the buildings are prefabricated steel, some of the older ones twisted and broken open, falling back into the ground. Half-frozen puddles line the wet and slush-filled gravel road.

I get to the terminal just as a flight is about to leave for Cambridge Bay. Ron, across the parking area, fuels the Beech 100 and then tows it with a pickup truck to the boarding area. Mario loads the baggage. Dan and Ranjit play ticket agent. There is a very large stuffed polar bear in the airport lobby, and a young woman from Vancouver, a paleobiologist who has been in the field studying fossil microbes in lake bed–mud core samples, takes what she calls the obligatory picture for friends back home.

When everyone boards and the Beech leaves Resolute, a small group gathers in Dan's office. There's Dan and Ranjit, a tall and lanky man named Jim Haffey who flies for the Polar Continental Shelf Project, a blond twenty-four-year-old new pilot named Rory MacNicol, and for a short while another Dan, Dan Mik-

konen, who simply calls himself Dan the Fuel Man. There's
a couch in the office, a small window, and three desk chairs.
There's a computer, and on one wall two radios. One is local,
to reach trucks and the hangar and the crew house. The other
is the HF radio. Most airplane radios are VHF, or very high frequency, because the clarity of the signal is high. High frequency
(without the "very") isn't nearly as clear, but the signal travels
much farther. This far north, that distance is essential.

Dan Minsky shows me the coffee. They are already talking
about yesterday's rescue, and I learn it wasn't people. It was
dogs. Sixteen dogs, some sleds, and other gear rescued from an
expedition because the dogs could no longer negotiate the de-
teriorating ice.

"Two Brits and two Canadians," Dan says. "They have a Web
site called Adventure Ecology, and they're doing it basically
to try to educate everyone about the changing ice conditions,
which is kind of ironic because now they are a victim of severely
changing ice conditions! I've been on the satellite phone with
them for almost a month, waiting for the ice to get into some
shape that would be an acceptable landing strip."

"So they just called and said, 'We have a strip,' and you guys
raced to get there?" I ask.

"That's pretty much it. We knew this was coming, so the
planning was done."

"The dogs, they were just all over each other," Rory says, "and
one of them had a cut and blood all over his face. Oh, it was
funny, because Russell, the dog handler, was about half the size
of any of the dogs in there, and he's jammed in there with sixteen, right? So all you could see is dogs and fur and blood, and
out of this mess comes Russ. When he landed, he's like, 'Whooo,
it's a long seven hours.'"

"You had a special dog handler?" I ask.

"Russell's actually an ex-fueler," Dan the Fuel Man continues.
"He was my right-hand man here."

"He's a local, from Grise Fiord, and so he grew up with dogs and has the experience to take care of them," Dan Minsky says. "Sixteen sled dogs in the back of a small plane really isn't something we want the pilots to deal with while they're flying. The expedition paid him a hundred dollars, he got a free flight, that kind of thing."

"How much did it cost them to do the rescue?" I ask.

"I can't tell you that," Dan says. "But ask me another question. Ask me how much it would cost for *you* to fly to 87 degrees north."

"How mu . . ."

"Forty grand."

"How much to fly me to the pole?"

"One hundred grand. Half an hour on the ground, max."

"You get that question a lot?"

"All the time."

"And the other sixty thousand is just profit?" I ask.

"No, for the pole we need two planes. Only one gets there, but the other stops short and carries some fuel for the return."

I ask about tricky approaches or hairy landings, and Jim turns to Rory, who has in his digital camera a video of an approach and landing they made a week ago at Haughton Crater, an asteroid-impact crater on Devon Island, the site of the Haughton-Mars Project, where people walk around in space suits and pretend they are on Mars. Serious science, actually. On the video there's nothing but white snow and ice, a few brown rocks sticking out in places. Depth perception and contrast seem impossible. But the plane touches down on the ice and glides to a stop as if it were the intention of the whole design. Showing the video, Rory never stops smiling.

"How do you tell what you're doing?" I ask.

"You do a couple ski drags on the ice and snow first, to test it before landing and to create contrast in the flat light," Jim says.

"But how do you do a ski drag in that light?"

Both Jim and Rory smile.

"Experience," Jim says.

Dan shows me a video he has on his computer of a Twin Otter taking off from a full stop in less than two lengths of the airplane. "There was a bit of a headwind," he says.

Pretty soon, our conversation gets back to the rescue. The men and women left behind are going to try to push on with their small sleds. But in truth, they are waiting for their own rescue now, which is really just a window wherein the plane can land and get them.

"This is the very latest, ever, that we've been that far out on the ice," Dan tells me.

"Was it a pretty hairy landing?" I ask.

"You'll have to ask Steve Kaizer—he was the pilot. I know it wasn't routine, but up here almost nothing is."

"So with the weather and the ice, who makes the decision to go or no-go?"

"We all make the decision together," Dan says. "But I suppose it finally falls to me. If the pilots say no, obviously I'm not going to say yes. But if the pilots say they can do it, it falls to me to actually approve the flight."

"And then you sit here, with the phone and the HF, to make sure they get home?"

"If something goes wrong, I'm the only one up here listening."

We get to talking about other things again. I learn all the food here arrives via Canada Post, carried by Kenn Borek and Canadian North airplanes, and that the jet fuel and aviation gas, as well as the diesel fuel for the electric generators, arrive via boat once a year. I learn Jim likes at least a meter of sea ice under his skis to support the plane for ice landings, and that he's been to both poles within six weeks of each other. I learn that Resolute used to be the second-busiest airport in Canada in the 1970s, when oil exploration was in high gear.

Dan tells a story about a guy who flew a Pilatus, a large and expensive single-engine airplane, up to Grise Fiord and didn't see or didn't care that it was a restricted approach. There are large hills at the ends of both runways, and a ditch at one end as well. He came in too hot and too steep, and apparently a number of people in town saw how he was coming in and started screaming because they knew he would crash. He made the landing, however, with his nose wheel on the edge of the ditch.

"Now he's probably telling the story of how good a pilot he is and how he made this impossible landing," I say.

"Yeah," Dan says. "And it was cold and his hands were numb and, and, and . . ."

I have to get back to the Narwhal, but before I go I ask Dan one private question. "Is this good work?" I ask. "Staying up till six in the morning, sitting in this office, listening to the radio to get the rescue crew home?"

* * *

The flight to Grise Fiord is ready at six. Steve Kaizer, the pilot, who yesterday flew the mission to rescue the dogs, and Rory, still so seemingly thrilled to be here, tow the plane to the fuel stop and then the terminal. The Twin Otter they pull up is not painted the dramatic red and black with lightning-bolt Kenn Borek colors, though. This one is off-white, with blue stripes down the side. The tail number is c-gpao, c for Canada, pao for Pan Arctic Oil, the company that sold the plane to Kenn Borek Air. The skis that were attached to the wheels yesterday are gone.

The bags and the cargo are loaded, but in the terminal a young Inuit man needs to fly to Grise Fiord and doesn't have a ticket or any other information, doesn't know who is supposed to pay. A guy from Nunavut Power offers his credit card and a guarantee. Dan takes the number, will use it only if some other arrangement isn't worked out. It's a casual deal. Things like this, he tells me, just get sorted out a little bit later, and it's all fine in the end.

Steve comes in the building and Dan introduces us, but there's no time to talk. We board, this time I get to sit in the far back with the guy from Nunavut Power, and at 6:37 the power levers get pushed forward and we are under way. If I didn't know better, I'd swear the forward roll to rotation and takeoff measures less than 300 feet. And the Otter has a pretty steep climb.

There are reasons this plane has the reputation it has. According to a spec sheet, at maximum weight, sea level, standard air pressure, and no wind (the universal setup for measuring airplane performance), a 300 series Twin Otter DHC-6 needs only 700 feet to take off using a short-field technique. In a normal takeoff, it needs only 860 feet. (By comparison, a new Beech 90GT needs 2,392 feet for a takeoff roll. The little two-seat Cessna 152 that I fly needs 750 feet.) It can land in 515 feet, or less. It can climb at 1,600 feet per minute, and has a ceiling of 26,700 feet, though it's not a pressurized plane and the crew and passengers would need supplemental oxygen. It's not really a fast plane—cruise at 10,000 feet is only 182 knots. But stall speed with full flaps is a very slow 58 knots. There are two Pratt and Whitney turboprop engines, each with three blade propellers, and the props can be put in full reverse, which is a hell of a way to stop.

In other words, the Twin Otter can carry a lot, in and out of tight places, and it's as stable as granite. It services the Arctic and Antarctic, and serves as an amphibious air taxi in the Maldives. If you're going someplace difficult, dangerous, or just plain screwy, you want a Twin Otter.

Cornwallis Island is still mostly snow covered. Patches of brown dirt and rock show through at bluffs and cliffs. The guy from Nunavut Power, Robert Sagades, tells me there are a lot of fossils here, especially in the North. And there's a petrified swamp forest just off the coast of Cornwallis, on Axel Heiberg Island. Robert is Caucasian, married to an Inuit woman from Grise Fiord. He's traveling with his mother-in-law, an old and small woman sitting in front of him, as well as a nephew or two sitting at windows. "She can tell you anything about this land," he says. "Anything at all. She just finished a 2,000-kilometer snowmobile trek."

The cloud deck below us grows thick and persistent, and I can't see anything on the ground. Robert says, "If it was a clear day, your jaw would drop for an hour and a half going north and an hour and a half going back south—all the glaciers and the ice caps. There's year-round open water just off of Devon Island, and just east of us there's the Devon crater." I try to imagine Jim and Rory landing there, the smile on Rory's face.

Soon enough, though, there's a break in the clouds. We are over Wellington Channel, just crossing over onto Devon Island, and I realize Robert is not kidding. The place really is jaw-droppingly beautiful. Snow-covered mountains and hills, valleys, what looks like rivers of snow and ice. Where we pass over a coast, valleys cut into cliff faces make the land look like paws resting on the ice.

We pass over the coast of Devon Island and out over Jones Sound.

"If you go out on the ice," Robert tells me, "stay away from the icebergs trapped in the sea ice."

"Why is that?" I ask.

"Icebergs go up and down with the tides, and that makes open water near the edges. Where there's open water, there are seals. Where there are seals, there are polar bears."

"This is good to know," I say.

Ellesmere Island comes up on our left side, and we parallel the coast heading east. Snowfields and glaciers reach from the top of coastal cliffs back toward the northern horizon. Robert calls out the names of each fjord, and when he can't remember he taps his mother-in-law on the shoulder and she replies without looking. Walrus Fiord. Goose Fiord. Harbour Fiord. The Heim Peninsula. Land Slip Island.

We begin our approach, and in the back of my head I hear a warning I copied from the Web site of the Canadian Owners and Pilots Association (COPA): "Only operators with considerable experience should use this aerodrome at all. It is a short one way strip with a curved approach path, normally only used by Twin Otters. If landing is not assured by the red overshoot bars then overshoot immediately—left climbing turn to 187T. PAPI lights are aimed 15 degrees right of runway. Caution high terrain all around. Nearest COPA Flight: a very long way away."

I've heard stories about this approach. Most of them told in a kind of nonchalant tone. Yes, the stories go, this is the only curved approach remaining in the world, and yes, this is a place where you really don't want anything to go badly, but you get used to it. From my seat in the back, I'm too far away and too low to get a good visual picture of the runway coming into view and the changing perspective, but I can see the mountain. I can see the mountain that fills the view from the cockpit window. From my point in the back, there is no sky above this rock, and no water below. Just a hillside, right in front of us, each detail becoming sharper every second we fly.

I watch the coast approaching out the left window and can see the town in front of us. We descend, and just as we cross the coast we bank to the left, level off, flare, and the main wheels kick up gravel. The landing roll is very short. Still, all I can see out the cockpit window is hillside and rock. We back-taxi on the runway and pull off to the small yellow-brown terminal building. On the other side of the chain-link fence, what I assume are families have gathered to welcome or say good-bye. Steve and Rory help linemen off-load the mail and cargo. Large boxes of Old Dutch potato chips, toilet paper. When one of the boxes of potato chips breaks open and a few of the individual bags fall on the ground, one of the linemen calls out with a laugh, "Hey! That's our survival food." And there's a touch of reality in that comment, too. This is as far north as the mail goes in North America, and most of that mail here is food. What they don't hunt from the land, they get from the air.

I walk away from the airplane and onto the runway to take some pictures, and for the first time I see a row of graves just outside the airport fence, not very far up the gravel beach. There are small crosses at the head of each stone-covered rise. But no one I ask seems to know whom they belong to. Although I don't know it yet, no one in Resolute will know those graves either. But the question will persist, and I will eventually get an e-mail from Dan.

So I was talking to a couple captains the other night and it seems that those graves at the end of the runway in Grise mark the remains of a Scottish expedition that ended up lost and stuck in the ice, having to winter over at that point some perished and the remaining crew buried them and returned home in the spring. I briefly checked into this but nobody could tell me the name of the ship or what year exactly this took place, however that seems to be the story behind the graves. Don't know if you can find anything out about it but I've seen similar graves (of Scottish whalers/explorers) along the north/eastern coast of Baffin Island.

One of the locals here tells me that Inuit from down on Baffin were with the expedition—a young woman and her husband who were offered rewards for "guiding" the expedition further north. I suppose they were responsible for the majority of the crew's survival that winter and it is rumored that their child was actually born in Europe. They returned to Baffin the next year (or sometime after) with their child but continued relations with the Scottish whalers that came to Baffin each year (many old whaling camps existed around Broughton Island, where I used to live so I found this pretty interesting). I was also told that this story was cited to the Inuit that were displaced from the south in convincing them that Inuit had been to Grise Fiord before. Supposedly those graves contain Inuit items from the two guides as they too paid their respects to the dead crew-members. That's all I managed to find out—hope it helps . . . not sure how true all of it is but you know how stories like this go.

"Stories like this," I will think. Exploration, adventure, and risk. There are reasons for the smile on Rory's face, and the peculiar thrill there is in sitting in a small office listening to an HF radio, bringing some crew home on jet fuel and hope.

Here in Grise Fiord, on this day, I watch Steve talk to a man who is bringing him a polar bear skin. It's not cured yet, just flesh and fur wrapped in a blue tarp, but he takes it with a smile and stuffs it in the nose of the airplane. Soon enough, it will decorate some floor or room.

We board again. Schoolkids and two teachers fill the plane. They are from Resolute, and have been on a field trip to Grise Fiord. The teacher tells me they are getting ready for a trip down to Halifax. She says this is a practice for the chaperones.

We take off the opposite way we landed, back out over Jones Sound, and I strain to see anything at all around the entrapped icebergs. But the clouds soon return, and I can't see a thing below us. Above us, the sun is bright and the sky is clear. When we get to Resolute, the ceiling has dropped to maybe 250 feet above ground level. But the landing is faultless, and soon enough everyone is where they want to be and Steve and I are settled in Dan's office, strong coffee in hand.

"Ninety-nine percent of the world," I say, "you're not on their radar. They've got no idea . . ."

"That this is happening," Steve finishes for me.

* * *

Steve Kaizer looks like the kind of guy who would be a great middle linebacker. He stands a thick five foot eight or nine, has a round face with a goatee and a beginning beard, an easy smile. He is thirty years old. He wears a black flight suit and a baseball cap. He would look odd, I think, in an airline captain's uniform, strolling through some airport with a little set of wheeled luggage behind him. But he seems to be made for a bush plane.

"I grew up in a small town in northern Ontario," he tells me. "And since I was eight years old I knew what I wanted to do with my life. I wanted to fly airplanes. My first lesson was when I went to flight college in Sault Sainte Marie, Ontario. I could never afford to do the private-pilot thing on my own. I was living in the Northwest Territories for my first job, and had a lot of friends that were working for Borek, and it was time for a change, time for a pay raise, see the world and get paid for it."

"Is that what attracted you to the company?" I ask. "The fact that this is just sort of on the edge?"

"If it's remote, if it's cold, if it's too hot, if it's nowhere else, nobody wants to go, chances are we have a plane there somewhere," he says. "But no, I think it was more just for the work part, the lifestyle. I had enough of actually living in the North full-time, so I wanted to live down South and still work up here. Because I still like to work up here. I love it, actually."

"Three weeks on and three weeks off is a good deal?" I ask.

"That's the rule, but it's a tough one to rely on. In the summertime we're really busy up here, and we can only fly in our Twin Otter up to 150 hours in our three weeks. We have a max of fourteen hour–duty days, fourteen hours of flying, fifteen if we get an extra hour's rest in there. So sometimes we'll get to

150 hours before our three weeks is up, so we have no choice but to go home, or have five consecutive days off to reset that time. So, if I'm on my time off and somebody up working times out before their time, I might get called. The three-in, three-out is nice on paper, but really it's 'Get the work done.'"

"You were engaged once. Is the schedule what killed it?"

"That was part of it," he says, sadly, "but not everything."

"Tell me about yesterday's story," I say. "The dog rescue. Are you the guy that if there's a really screwy flight, they're going to call you, or did you just happen to be on the rotation?"

"I just happened to be on the base machine. That's pretty normal stuff up here. It was a little different because that was the latest we've landed out that far on the ice in the season . . ."

"Latest?" I ask. "As in ever, in history?"

"As far as I know, yeah. But it doesn't really mean anything. We have three groups out there right now, two coming from the Russian side to the pole, then to Canada. That's a long trek in itself, and ice is actually pretty bad this year, so that's why we're kind of behind schedule. For that trip—I'm here, here's a trip, there you go."

"They have the satellite phone, radio, and a GPS," I say. "They could tell you right where they were, so you wouldn't have any trouble finding them. But you didn't know when you took off if the weather was going to be any good when you got there?"

"Yeah, it was a long flight. I mean, seven hours' flight time just to get there. And the weather up here, as you can see, can change so quick."

"That's a long way past the range of a Twin Otter."

"Well, we have a fuel cache in Eureka. From there we go to a place called Ward Hunt Island. It's right on the north coast of Ellesmere. And we refuel there again, and put some barrels of fuel in the plane too. From there we went up to 86.5 degrees north and got the dogs. Came back to Ward Hunt, refueled, flew to Eureka, refueled again, and then back here."

"How much did you carry with you when you left Ward Hunt? How many barrels? How many pounds?"

"When we left? I don't know—I'd have to look that up. Enough to get there and back, plus a lot of fudge factor. We've got to make sure—and that's the real trick about the northern flying. We don't have fuel everywhere. We don't have airports everywhere. The weather changes so dramatically, and it can be so localized."

"So what do you do," I ask, "when you've got no alternates and you've got to get there and get back to this one airport? What if Ward Hunt was unlandable when you got back?"

"It was close to unlandable when we got back." Steve pauses and looks at me. I wait for him to go on. "It was good enough for us to get in," he says.

"What was it?" I ask.

"Okay. When we landed, it was probably twenty feet, and a quarter mile."

Steve smiles at me, and there is a part of me that wonders about exaggeration. But I've also been standing outside, and seen this weather. Clouds, twenty feet above the ground, I think. Visibility below that twenty feet, not more than a quarter mile into the distance. The top of the Twin Otter's fuselage is nine feet, eight inches. The top of the tail is nineteen feet, seven inches. When Steve's window offered a view, his wheels were only twelve feet off the ground.

"And there's nothing on the ground to help the approach," I say.

"Just a frozen lake. But it wasn't completely overcast. It wasn't completely cloudy. It was kind of in and out. When we went through there on the way north, it was just localized right around the island, maybe in a two-mile radius, clear as a bell everywhere else. By the time we got back, everywhere was foggy, all the fjords, everything. But that's fun," he says. "That's what we do. Everybody's used to beacons and waypoints and all that stuff down South, but when you do it up here, it's GPS and it's visual and it's maps."

"Did you have fuel to carry on to Eureka if you couldn't get into Ward Hunt?"

"Not to Eureka. Polar Shelf does a lot of work, and they have fuel caches all over the place. They're not Kenn Borek's fuel caches, but we don't use them and not replace."

"And actually, Polar Shelf contracts with Kenn Borek for the pilots and planes," I say.

"Yeah, it's understandable. And they expect it. For anybody that's up there working, fuel is very important. So as long as you can replace it, then they don't really care. We did have enough fuel to get to Alert."

"Could you just divert there," I ask, "without the military clearance? They're not going to say you can't land or we'll shoot you down."

"They can deny us, but they wouldn't. We didn't have too many other options to go to. You always have to plan. You just can't plan for your trip. You have to plan for your trip and then the worst-case scenario."

"But this flight went pretty well."

"Yeah, it went without a hitch. The only problem was trying to get back into Ward Hunt after coming back from up North. I think I had four missed approaches on that one."

I try to imagine Steve bringing the Twin Otter into Ward Hunt. Low clouds, no real visibility. If he misses here, he has to go hunting for fuel. This is a landing site he knows, but he still has to see it. First approach—nothing, and so a go-around. Second approach—nothing. How many times would you bring the plane in, I wonder, reaching for the ground with the gingerliness of a small bird, hoping you can see what's ahead early enough to use it? Third approach—nothing. When do you say, "I can't do this," and move on to something else? When do you say, "Oh, hell, I'm going to do this anyway"?

"Tell me about the landing on the ice, and the dogs. What do you need for a landing like that?"

"It really depends," Steve says. "There are so many variables. The surface. The kind of snow. If it's wet, if it's dry, if it's hard. It really makes a difference. Up there it was maybe two to three inches of wet snow, which is really kind of sluggish in takeoff. But you taxi back and forth and pack it down and take off in your tracks."

"You did a ski drag before you landed?"

"We always do. We did two drags, and pretty much in the first drag I was convinced we'd be no problem."

"How you do that? Just keep the nose high and drag the tail?"

"The idea behind it is to put some weight on the surface and kind of feel the strip. You get kind of an idea of how long it is and how rough it is. The wheel skis are not really designed to take a lot of beating, so the surface has to be pretty smooth to land on it. We kind of drag it to feel it out, to see if there are any big hummocks or ice kind of things that you land on. You do that a few times, and each time you come down you maybe put a little more weight or go a little slower."

"That's a lot of finesse for an airplane that size."

"Max weight's 12,500 pounds. But it's designed to do exactly that, so I mean it's a very stable airplane."

"Tell me the details, the step by step," I ask. "I have no idea how I would do this in the 152. Tell me how you get an airplane set up so lightly you can feel the quality of the ice in your hands and feet."

Steve looks at me. There is a difference between knowing a procedure and feeling it in your lungs and muscles. You can explain some things, in tremendous and exacting detail, and never get at the heart of what it's really like. But the words are still a pretty good doorway.

"Each captain has their own way of doing things," he says, "but this is how I usually do it. First pass is usually 10 degrees of flap and 90 knots, about 25-PSI torque and props in cruise, for a visual inspection of the surface and to pick a line between sastrugi and other obstacles. Once I find a line that suits my needs for length, I will drag the main skis with 20 degrees of flap and about 70 knots. Sometimes I'll do this twice. Next is full flap, 37.5 degrees, and 60–65 knots. This will give you a good idea if the strip will be long enough to stop on. Remember, no brakes on skis! Then I'll do a dry run where I'll have the aircraft set up for an actual landing scenario. This means putting the aircraft behind the power curve in a full flap and props at full fine configuration and airspeed hovering just above the stall. I'll drag all three skis on the surface and run the length of the landing area before applying takeoff power and going around. If I believe everything is satisfactory, then the next time will be the same configuration and a prop selection on full reverse upon touchdown. Depending on the type of surface I'm landing on, it depends on what I do after I land as well. On bare ice I'll slow down to a crawl and very slowly taxi around, stopping and starting three times. I do this to cool the skis down. If you just land on ice and stop, the skis will melt the ice just enough to weld the skis after they cool down, so the next time you start up and apply power to taxi, you will go nowhere. Kind of embarrassing if someone's looking! We carry a large block of wood and a twenty-pound sledgehammer to break the skis from the surface. If on soft, wet, or deep snow I'll taxi back and forth along the landing area many times to pack down the surface. These types of landing surfaces create lots of drag on the skis and will extend your takeoff slide considerably, even to the point where it might be impossible to become airborne with the length of ski-way available."

"That's still a lot of finesse," I say, "to land on a surface that you're not sure about. If the guys out there are wrong and the ice is only three inches thick, you don't want to go water-skiing. You've got to still be at flying speed."

"Yeah . . . , you're . . . , well, it's . . . , I mean, you could look at different cues you can use. The color of the ice. If it's broken up, you can see how much. If it's turned 90 degrees, you can see kind of how thick it is, and you can kind of gauge to see where the waterline is to where the top of the ice is."

"Did you do this all yesterday?"

"Yep."

"How many approaches did you make, just for observation?"

"Well, we did two, but I was looking at the ice structure along the way, and big orbits. It looked pretty much all the same kind of uniform mass, just tracks, and the pan they were on sure looked clearly usable. They took one of their ski poles, down between the cracks, and they couldn't get the bottom."

"What do you need to hold the airplane?"

"It depends . . ."

"What would the manual say?"

"At least three feet. I mean, you can get lower, like two. But it's been warm up there. This morning's temperature is like plus four, so ice weakens. You could have thick ice and still not."

"You keep the engines running when you're down?"

"Sometimes, if it's remote or real sketchy sort of thing, or it's an emergency. That wasn't an emergency; didn't have to get there. It was clearly a good pan of multiyear ice there, so I didn't have a problem shutting it down. But we did brief on the way there, that if it was kind of sketchy, I would sit there with the engines running, flaps at takeoff setting, we'd go in the back, open up the doors, throw their kit out, throw the dogs in, and go. Minimum time. But it wasn't that bad, not nearly that bad."

"How long were you actually on the ice?"

"Twenty-five minutes or so. It was still pretty quick."

"And what time did you take off?" I ask.

Steve looks at me and smiles. "Fourteen hours before we got back."

I smile back at him. There are rules, I think, and there is work to be done.

"What was Russell thinking through all this?" I ask.

Steve laughs loudly. "I don't know. He was having a good time. It was his first time up there. He was okay. Except for the dogs in the back fighting."

* * *

Three teams on the ice. No one talks about the one heading toward Russia. Yet there are two on the phone to Resolute. The Adventure Ecology team wants to press on, but in truth they already know they will need to be rescued. The ice is breaking up. The second team, at 87 degrees north, needs supplies. No landing on this one. This will be an airdrop of plastic barrels that hold what they need. Tomorrow morning, Steve and Rory and a flight engineer will take C-GPAO to Eureka again, to Ward Hunt again, and north again. In Eureka, they will take the cargo doors off the airplane to make the airdrop easier. Steve's been to the South Pole with Kenn Borek, but he's never been to the North Pole. Yesterday's 86.5 degrees north was a personal record. Tomorrow, if the weather is good, 87 degrees north will be the new mark. But this team too knows they cannot finish their walk over the ice to solid ground. Somehow, they will need collection.

"These guys," Steve tells me, meaning the second team, as we are leaving the office, "are a lot worse. I've got some pictures, a lot of open water. I think they're completely discouraged. If they get through that section, they're a little bit better. They're looking to get pulled out because they heard we went into the other place, which, by the way, was a miracle this pad of ice was there, and so now they want us to fly in to get them. We gave them coordinates where there is good ice, but by the time they get there, it could be useless."

"What are their options going to be if you can't land?" I ask, as we stop outside the building and into a small snow shower.

"Not everyone who makes that trip makes it," he says.

* * *

Sunday afternoon at the airport in Resolute is deceptively quiet. At the Narwhal, helicopter pilots and mechanics and others watch TV and rest in the deep chairs. Every now and then, someone plays a game of pool. The sky clears, then closes in, then clears again, over and over. Walking the wet and muddy gravel road between the Narwhal and the terminal building, I can sometimes see all the way down the slope and out over Resolute Bay, sea ice glistening in the distance, and sometimes I cannot see more than half a mile in front of me. Snow showers come and go with the clouds.

Somewhere north of here, Steve and Rory and an engineer are flying C-GPAO to 87 degrees north to kick some barrels and supplies out to a polar expedition. Jim Haffey and whomever he's flying with have taken off for the Polar Continental Shelf Project to retrieve some fuel barrels that were left earlier, a half-dozen off-strip landings today.

Dan is working in the Kenn Borek office, the real focus of his attention the HF radio again. Ranjit wanders in and out, listening to the radio as well.

"Do relationships work up here?" I ask. "They've got to be incredibly difficult, because I've yet to meet anyone who says they work. Steve tells me he used to be engaged."

"New guys come out," Dan says, "and the biggest joke is, 'Oh yeah, my girlfriend this and that . . .' Good luck. 'Cause you're up here three weeks, and you make plans for your anniversary or birthday and then you get stuck. So with our work getting done, there's always priorities. These guys don't get home often. Even myself. This is week five out of the three-week rotation. It's actually the same for those guys too."

"This is week five, and you're two weeks overdue," I say. "Is there someone sitting in Toronto thinking, 'I'm supposed to be up there to replace him'?"

"No, we're short of base managers now. My replacement is in Cambridge Bay. The other guy there is somewhere else. Usually, I get out on three weeks on time, but weather can always keep you here. I go out on Mondays or Fridays as well. So say I'm supposed to go out on a Monday and the weather's no good. I'm here until Friday. Or say my replacement gets weathered out, then I'm up here anyway because you can't leave the base unattended."

"If tomorrow's flight is weathered out," I say, "you don't just sit here until Friday. You just wait for the first window and go then, right?"

"Not necessarily. It depends."

"I fly out tomorrow. It's going to be great weather tomorrow."

"The more you say that, the worse it gets."

Dan lights another cigarette, and I pour another cup of coffee. It's too early in the mission for Steve to call in yet. This is just pacing time. When Ranjit comes in, Dan asks if I'd like to see the hangar, so we get up and head toward one of the pickup trucks.

"I've seen a woman once," he says on the way. "A very good story, actually. This woman came up here to have a forty-five-minute meeting in Grise Fiord. She came up from some branch of the federal government down South. She had no desire to be in the Arctic. She came up and was not interested in anything. She's like, 'This is it? It's ugly.' And I guess in a way she's right. She was just cold and fed up, and we canceled three Grise Fiord flights because of the weather. And we have no place for rescheduling because in July and August we're basically booked all month long. Right? You have a charter today, and I say, 'We can't go because of weather.' You say, 'Okay, tomorrow.' I say, 'No, maybe in the next week or two,' because we can't just push every flight back one day. We wait for another weather cancellation. It's a big juggling act. So anyway, she came up and she was just livid, *livid*, so we fly her up because she wanted to go up on the Wednesday and back on Saturday. She finally goes up a week late. Then we try to come back in, and we miss. We can't land there. We go up there, and we overshoot the approach and come back. Can't see a thing, right? Then we try ten out of the next fourteen days. We couldn't get in. And we have food sitting in our hangars, spoiling. And we have mail. We have about three planeloads. We have about twenty passengers on both ends looking to move, right? And they're sold out. Then we have about fourteen hours' worth of charter flying every single day. I'm sitting here, and I can't get into Grise Fiord. The community is out of milk, out of eggs, cheese. They're waiting for medicine. There was a rabies thing going on, and we had all the vaccines here and everything. And this poor woman, she's three weeks into her three-day trip. We finally get in, bring her back here, and she misses the jet that's taking her out, the First Air jet. The jet couldn't get into Resolute, so that was another four days on top of that. So it's almost a month. And she was supposed to come up on the Wednesday, go to Grise, get off, and get to fly Saturday and go home on Saturday. It was almost a month. Just weather. It was just weather."

* * *

At the hangar, Ron and Mario are on the wings of the Beech 100, wiping it down with cleaner and rags. The Beech sits under a tent inside the hangar, "to save on what we have to heat," Dan says. One of the mechanics is looking at a fuel pump in the left engine. Outside the tent, the hangar is dark, and Dan shows me the sleds and other gear from the dog team stashed in a corner.

"When will Steve and Rory be out of radio range?" I ask.

"They're not going to be out of radio range," Dan says. "It's very possible that because of the solar activity I won't be able to reach them, but I'm the only one that follows these guys. I mean, anything north of here, they can't reach anyone else."

"They could reach Alert; they could reach Eureka."

"Alert is a private frequency and Eureka is only VHF, so they can only get Eureka within about eighty miles. So anywhere eighty miles north of Eureka, there's no communication except for here. In the high Arctic, I'd be willing to say we're the only ones that listen to this HF twenty-four hours a day. It's never off. And I've got one in the house too that I listen to. We can pick up planes as far west as Inuvik and as far south as Yellowknife. We picked up one of our planes in trouble in Sannikiluaq, in Hudson Bay, about a year and a half ago. All of the Borek planes that fly around in the Arctic know we're listening and will call us. Like, I get calls from planes flying out of Iqaluit all of the time. And I just relay information, telling people when they're coming home. Say they get somewhere and they have to divert. It's very important for us, because a lot of the time we are the ones responsible. And especially with the Twin Otters that are doing off-strip work, we need to know where those planes are. In the event that anything should happen, we are responsible for the planes. So I need to know exactly where that Otter is at all times, right? And when you do big trips, sometimes that includes calling in position reports."

"Is this a big trip?" I ask, nodding toward the HF radio.

"This is a long trip. This is a big trip."

* * *

An hour later, Dan, Ranjit, and I are back in the office, listening to the radio again, following Steve and Rory and their flight to 87 degrees north. When the phone rings, it's the expedition manager, the person back on the mainland somewhere who is in charge of the expedition out on the ice, calling to get an update.

Dan gives him the basics of where we are and what's going on. The plane was in Eureka, it was getting some work done on it, getting the doors off and such, and soon it should be out.

Dan hangs up with the expedition manager, and not a minute later c-gpao radios in to say they are airborne from Eureka. However, the radio transmission is static-filled and difficult, and we can hear Steve say he will call on his own satellite phone. But Dan radios back a "roger roger roger," telling Steve don't bother—we have the information we need.

Then the phone rings again, and it's the team on the ice, calling on their satellite phone, looking for an update. They give Dan their coordinates and ask for an estimated time of arrival (eta). Dan guesses it will be about two hours, but then the other phone line breaks in and rings too. Steve is on the satellite phone from the airplane. Again trouble with transmissions, solar activity causing interference, but Dan gives the coordinates to the airplane, gives an updated eta back to the guys on the ice, and passes information between the two groups about how the drop zone should be marked.

Sitting on the office couch, watching Dan pace back and forth, I can't help but think this is an undiscovered movie set. The drama, I think, is thick in the air.

"Roger roger roger," Dan says to a transmission. His voice is measured and clear.

"Unreadable, unreadable, unreadable," he says, again in a measured and clear voice, to let someone in the distance know their transmission was not understood in Resolute.

I ask Dan and I ask Ranjit, "Is this just another day in the office?" They say, "Yeah, we do this all the time."

We sit and drink coffee. The hf radio is turned up, but no one is transmitting. Somewhere a good bit north of us, there are people looking into the vast sky for a very small airplane. And there are people in an airplane scanning the vast ice for a small group of people.

Latitude: 87°00′45″ N.
Longitude: 73°07′49″ W.

* * *

"7–6. 7–6. Papa Alpha Oscar." Even though he sounds very far away, Steve's voice is unmistakable in the radio speaker.

"PAO, PAO, 7–6. Go ahead," Dan replies.

Papa Alpha Oscar is C-GPAO. 7–6 is Resolute.

"Unreadable. Unreadable. Drop in place! Drop complete! On our way back to Eureka. Estimate, ah, approximately two hours, four five minutes. Two hours, four five minutes."

"Roger roger roger. Anything on empties at Ward Hunt Island? Empties on Ward Hunt? How on that?"

Dan speaks slowly, enunciating every syllable. Except "How on that?" sounds like one word, "Howonthat?" It's a gentle question, I think, at the end of his transmission. Did you get that? he's asking. Did you hear me? Everything okay?

"Unreadable, unreadable. Ah, PAO out."

"Roger, roger, roger," he says, his voice a bit saddened.

"You say that the same way, slowly, every time," I say.

"Even if he can't understand what you're saying," Dan says, "say 'roger, roger, roger' three times. Everyone can hear that. And you try to say it the same way every time, right? He can understand that. In a situation like that, the unreadables, you want to break it down to basics. If he wants to call me on the sat phone, by my three rogers he knows everything's okay on my end, that I've got all the information. They know, if they couldn't reach me—like, say he couldn't hear me at all, which is not unreadable, it's like he can't hear me at all—he'll transmit blind. He'll call a few times and I'll try to call back, and he'll be like, '7–6, this is Papa Alpha Oscar transmitting blind.'"

"You said that earlier," I say. "He could hear you fine, but you couldn't hear him."

"That's right. And it was vice versa on the sat phone. Because of the sound of the engine, I couldn't hear anything he was saying. I asked him how he was picking me up, when I said, 'How do you read me?' and he said, 'Five by five.'"

"Do you think the expedition will retrieve all the barrels and get all set before they call you?" I ask.

"They might make sure they're finding everything that was there."

As if on cue, the telephone rings and it's the expedition team. Then the phone rings again, and it's someone else.

"Hey, Lonnie, standby one," Dan says to the expedition team.

"Hey, Kevin," he says to the other person. "It's actually the expedition so I can find out if everything went okay. Yeah, about two and a half hours to Eureka and then whatever this change-over is to get everything done and ready to come back. Yeah, I know it is. I'm going to talk with them. I was unreadable with them on the radio, and I'm going to pass that message along, hoping he'll be on the sat phone. Anyway, that's the guy on the ice, so I'll take that and let you know."

"Hey, Lonnie, go ahead!" Dan's voice is louder and more enthusiastic. In the office, Ranjit and I can hear only one side of the satellite-phone conversation. "Okay, roger that. Everything's intact, and you collected everything? . . . Right on. Right on. Did they hit the mark okay, or you have to go running for it? . . . Right on. That's good to hear. Makes me proud. . . . Right on, right on, I'm glad to hear it. . . . Yeah, right on, I talked to John about getting some pictures, so I'm glad they buzzed you a couple times. That's perfect. They'll probably have some great shots. . . . Yeah, perfect. And listen, you guys take care of each other, and good luck. . . . Yeah, absolutely, feel free if you need anything or even a pair of eyes on a sat shot, you let me know, give me a shout here. I'll talk to John about how you're doing and check on the Web site there. So best of luck to both of you. . . . Okay, no problem whatsoever. We'll talk to you then."

The HF radio comes back to life, Steve's voice on the radio again.

"Papa Alpha Oscar, 7–6. Go ahead," Dan says.

"7–6, Papa Alpha Oscar, transmitting in the blind," Steve says. "Eureka, zero one one fife. Eureka, zero one one fife."

"One, one, fife," in radio talk, is "one one five." Zulu time, or Greenwich mean time.

"Roger roger roger," Dan says. "Copy all. Copy all. How are you reading me?"

Silence.

"I don't think they can hear at all," Dan says to me.

"They put up two bags," Dan says. He means garbage bags at the drop site, to mark the drop zone, to give some contrast on the never-ending ice sheet. "And they just smoked the bags both times."

"I wanted to go," I say.

"So did I," says Ranjit.

"Hell, so did I," says Dan.

* * *

The barrels have been dropped, and Steve and Rory and C-GPAO are on their way back. But there is still work to be done. Dan calls a woman named Bonnie on the telephone. Bonnie, from what I can tell, is in Eureka.

"Hello, Bonnie? It's Dan at Borek. How are you?" Again, Ranjit and I can only hear one side of the conversation. "I'm keepin' out of trouble. . . . Thank you. . . . I don't believe it. Not after the pictures I saw. . . . No, don't get shy. I'll just hear you love trouble. There's nothing wrong with that, Bonnie. . . . Right on. How's your weather doing up there? . . . Yeah, right on, that's good. You guys are back to your usual forty-mile visibility? . . . Ah, that's perfect. . . . Looking for, yeah, I think they were worried about it being a little hairy getting back in there. . . . But no, that's good news. See if I can't reach the boys in a little bit and let them know. They're on their way back to you, mission accomplished and all that.... Yeah, PAO. I've got an ETA off the HF.... No, that's good. They say 0–1–1–5. So unless that changes or anything, if that does change, I'll let you know, Bonnie.... Okay, thanks for all your help. Talk to you later."

We pour coffee again. The HF radio takes the next turn. It begins to hum and make clicking noises, and Dan looks at me and Ranjit.

"That's Jim Haffey," he says.

"How do you know before he says anything?" I ask.

"Bravo Bravo Victor! Hello, it's 7–6," Dan calls out.

"Ah, good afternoon, it's Jim and me. We're just wondering if maybe you can call Raymond in Grise Fiord and get a weather observation, please?"

"Tell Jim, Raymond is no longer there," Dan says. "I will get weather for Grise Fiord for you, however."

"Okay, standing by."

"Did I call it or did I call it?" Dan asks me.

"How did you know?"

"That's the sound of his radio tuning up."

Dan calls Grise Fiord and gets the weather, then transmits it to Jim and his crew.

"Winds from the southeast 5 to 10 knots. Visibility 10 statute miles. Light snow. Sky conditions 1,500 scattered, 12,000 overcast from a ground observation. How on that?"

"Copy copy copy. Thank you very much. How's it look out there—pretty stormy?"

"Yeah," Dan says. "It's comin' down now, Jim, a little bit of fog here. We'll pull up the latest here for you, but I'm guessing it's about a mile now."

"Okay, roger."

"You want to stand by for the METAR?"

"Yeah, I guess in five or so minutes," Jim calls.

"Okay. I'll be standing by on 5–2. What are your intentions? Where are you going?"

"We're on the way to Resolute from Eureka right now, 162 miles back. 0–0–0–5 at about one hour and ten minutes."

"Roger, 0–0–0–5. Yeah, we'll check that weather for you in ten here, Jim. Give me a shout when you're ready."

* * *

So many people, I think, in the office with the three of us. Dan, Ranjit, myself. But also Steve and Rory and the engineer riding in the back of c-GPAO. Add to this the guys on the ice, and the expedition manager. Then add Bonnie in Eureka, and the Borek employee in Grise Fiord. Add Jim Haffey and his crew. And someone named Kevin.

Just offstage, add Ron and Mario and Rhonda and Joan, all the helicopter pilots and mechanics, and even the pilots of the two military helicopters that showed up last night, though no one is certain why they are here, or where the pilots are. Add all the employees of Canada Post. Add the cook in the double-breasted white jacket.

Earlier, at the hangar, Mario invited me to have dinner at the crew house, and so when things get quiet on the radio I wander over. The crew house is really two or three mobile homes pressed together, looking lived-in, and very comfortable. Mario, I learn, is a wonderful cook. Dinner is a hot dish of spicy sausage and peppers and onions and tomatoes, with a side of brussels sprouts. Every single bit of the meal, I know, has been mailed here from somewhere else. Mario puts a tremendously large portion on my plate, and I feel honor-bound to finish it.

After dinner, Ron breaks out some charts and maps, and we spend hours going over possible flights, places they have been, places we would all like to go. I cannot get over how lines on a pilot's chart that show magnetic deviation, the difference between a compass heading and the reading on a magnetic compass caused by the simple fact that the geographic and magnetic North Poles are not in the same place, which are ruler straight on every map I have ever seen, curve and whirl their way toward the magnetic North Pole on the Arctic charts. It's art, I think, like so much up here. Masquerading as something else.

* * *

Monday morning, the flight from Resolute back to Iqaluit offers fine weather and views to match any siren. Just for effect, I believe, the fog was thick at our scheduled departure time, and I worried that we would not leave. But then it lifted, we said our good-byes, and the Beech 100 carried just a few of us away.

Pond Inlet, with the mountains across the strait, is as pretty as everyone claims. Ron and Mario and I chat about everything and nothing, and the flight goes fast. In Iqaluit, I meet with Joan and talk about the past few days. It turns out she actually hasn't met Mario yet, and when he shows up at her door I'm already there. I praise his flying and his cooking, and when I see him sometime later in the terminal, he asks me earnestly, "What did you say?"

Ron and Mario board new passengers, and one of them is a Twin Otter pilot for Kenn Borek, heading up to Resolute for his three-week rotation.

"Are you a Twin Otter pilot?" Mario calls to him from behind the ticket counter.

"Yes, I am!" the man calls back.

"And you are not embarrassed to be seen in a Beechcraft?" Mario calls, smiling.

"Yes, I am!" the man smiles back, broadly.

I watch the taxi and takeoff, and a large part of me wishes I were back on that plane. But another plane will soon take me to Ottawa, where I will spend the night with friends, and tomorrow I will fly to Winnipeg and then drive home.

But I already know there are moments I will save. "This is a strange and original place," Dan told me once. "Coming up here, you meet a lot of strange and original people."

And there was Ranjit, outside the Kenn Borek office just after the supply drop at 87 degrees north was done. "What's this like, for you?" I asked him.

"Just another day at the office," he said, but his smile was huge.

And there was Steve, while we were talking about the Twin Otter. "It's a well-designed tank; it's a really tough airplane," he said. "As far as being able to work in the cold, the systems are—I don't think they were specifically designed, but just not as affected as some other more complicated systems. It's a very simple airplane; there's nothing complex there at all. It's an airplane: it's got two engines, and that's it. And that's why it's so popular in these remote regions."

Steve paused, and I could see a brightness come into his face.

"It's too bad we can't sit here more," he said. "In the summertime, when we've got the tundra tires on, there's this place by Pond Inlet. St. Joe's, I think. And it's in this river valley. The strip is only 600 feet long, on the inside of a river, and the walls are 300 feet vertical. So we have to go in turning around and then land."

This is fun, I think. This is what we do.

But most of all there is that question on the morning of the second day.

"Is this good work?" I asked. "Staying up till six in the morning, sitting in this office, listening to the radio to get the rescue crew home?"

Dan looked straight at me. He said, "This is the most dynamic, most fulfilling job I could possibly dream of."

2. Chasing Ivan

✳ ✳ ✳ ✳

Outside the visitor center at Keesler Air Force Base in Biloxi, Mississippi, the air is thick, hot, and humid. So humid I can feel my clothes sticking to my skin, the easy sweat on my forehead and neck. It's 3:07 in the morning, and a short distance away, the Gulf of Mexico, black under a moonlit sky, is smooth and untroubled. There are a few clouds, but nothing special or threatening yet. The waves, only bubbles as they break on the beach, would be measured in inches. A few people, late-night partiers, sit in a circle on the sand and laugh, their voices carrying easily in the still night air.

As I sit on the concrete steps, I hear a train approaching, its horn blowing at each roadway intersection. A guard at the gate, M-16 over her shoulder, calls to me when the train is near, and asks me if I'm Major Someone-or-Other. I cannot hear the name because of the horn, but I smile and assure her I am not. The train passes. The guard steps back into the guardhouse to talk with her partner. The night air remains thick and heavy.

A small car pulls up and parks at the visitor center. A man and a woman get out and then collect camera bags and backpacks from the backseat. The three of us have never met, but we smile, already knowing why the other is here. Chelsea Kenyon, I learn, is a meteorologist at KPLC television in Lake Charles, Louisiana. Her husband, Tom, is a cameraman. When they settle on the steps with me, all of us look down the road toward the Gulf of Mexico. We are waiting for one more camera crew, and we are waiting for the extraordinary. In just a few hours, we will be in an airplane, a wc-130. And that airplane will be in the rain bands, the winds, and then the eye of Hurricane Ivan.

Two days ago, I was more than fifteen hundred miles north of here, in Moorhead, Minnesota, where I live and where I teach. When I wasn't in class, I was stuck to the television and the Internet. Hurricane Ivan, a category 5 storm and already the sixth-strongest storm ever recorded, had left Jamaica in shambles and was bearing down on the Cayman Islands. No one knew when it would turn north. If it kept its track and moved through the Yucatán Channel, the water between the Yucatán Peninsula and Cuba, it would never cross land and never weaken before it ran into some high-pressure air and was pushed toward New Orleans, or Mississippi, or the panhandle of Florida. People were already dead and more were dying, and everybody who could get out of the way was getting out as fast as possible. But I jumped every time the cell phone rang. I wanted nothing more than to be in the heart of the thing.

I confess, to Chelsea and Tom here at the beginning, that my interest isn't really with the hurricane itself, although I have always loved storms. Growing up in Missouri and Illinois, every thunderstorm and tornado found me pressed against the windows or heading outside, just to see or feel the monster more closely. Living in New England and now in Minnesota, at the North Dakota border, I have come to love blizzards and their deep, lethal wind and cold and snow as evidence the earth is larger than even our grandest ambitions. And this love of storms has made me listen more earnestly when someone tells a story about being in one, and makes me read more carefully when some magazine prints an adventure.

But sometime long ago, thirty years or more, I do not remember when, I heard or read about the Hurricane Hunters, the men and women who fly their planes into the fury and then the eye of a hurricane, and a desire was fixed in my bones. If there was a way to get on one of those planes, I thought. If there was a way to fly *like that*.

When my father was much younger than I am now, he was a private pilot. My mother was a flight attendant for TWA. My father says, although I do not remember this, that when I was very young, one or two years old, and he was flying his Beechcraft Bonanza, a racy airplane with a V-tail, I would sometimes sit up front and help him fly. And there is a home movie of Christmas when I was in kindergarten that shows me wandering around the house in my foot-pajamas, with a tremendously large Styrofoam astronaut's helmet on my head. Apparently, I refused to take the thing off. Then, as well as now, I found every airplane beautiful and filled with grace. Then, as well as now, there were certain flights and missions that made me gasp. The x-15. Coast Guard helicopter rescues. Hurricane Hunters.

Another small car pulls to a stop at the visitor center, but this one comes from inside the base. A tall, good-looking black man wearing a camouflage uniform gets out and greets us.

"Mornin'," we all say.

"I'm Senior Airman Eaton," he says. "I'm your PA rep for today. Is everyone here?"

My mind does a quick code-breaking. PA rep: public affairs representative. Got it.

Chelsea and Tom and I look at each other. We've been told there are three crews. Eaton looks at me. "Where are you from?" he asks.

"Minnesota," I say. Eaton raises his eyebrows and smiles at me, then turns toward Chelsea and Tom.

"KPLC," she says. Eaton nods.

"So we're waiting for CNN," he says dryly. And everyone smiles.

We stand around for a few minutes and wonder if we should

go on and leave the CNN crew outside the gate. It's clear Eaton does not want to delay whatever is going to happen inside the base, and it's clear he also does not want to make a return trip to fetch the missing journalists. We load our backpacks and camera bags back into the cars and get ready to leave.

Finally, the others arrive. Another small car pulls fast into the parking lot and brakes hard to a stop. Two men get out. The reporter's name is Jason Bellini. Young and bright-smiled, he clearly thinks he's at the top of today's pecking order, while the rest of us haven't thought about pecking order at all. The cameraman he's brought along is Ben Blake. Also young, though quiet, he wears a brace on one arm. When I ask him what happened, Bellini interrupts to answer for him. "Skydiving! Can you believe it?" When Bellini turns away, Blake smiles.

I ride with Eaton, and the others pack their own cars. At the guardhouse, the soldiers with the M-16s check our driver's licenses, and then we are off.

* * *

The mission of the Fifty-third Weather Reconnaissance Squadron, the Hurricane Hunters, is straightforward. Their job is nothing less than to fly into the largest storm our planet produces, to fly a transect of the storm and cross the center of the eye as exactly as possible, all the while measuring the wind speed, wind directions, air pressure, and dew point, and to send that data to the supercomputers at the National Hurricane Center, where the meteorologists will try to predict where the storm is going, how it is changing, how long it will last, and how strong it's going to be. And, having done this, their mission is to do it again. And again. Four or five times per mission, from outer edge direct to the eye and out the other side.

The squadron is housed in an unspectacular building fronting the tarmac and then the runways. Ordinary glass doors open into a lobby. A hallway to the right leads to offices and work-rooms. Straight ahead and a bit to the left, doors lead to a large theater-style meeting room. Another hallway to the left leads to the coffee room, which holds a round table for smaller meetings or just conversation.

When we walk in, however, two things catch everyone's attention. Straight across the lobby another set of doors leads to the tarmac, and above them is a sign. Black background with large white letters and the insignias of the Air Force Reserve Command and the Hurricane Hunters, the sign reads: "Through these doors walk the world famous Hurricane Hunters." It's a bit of bravado and hype, and a bit of gravitas as well. On a wall to the left there is a mural, planes flying through blue skies and soft white clouds. The wc-130, large and center, is surrounded by the b-25 Mitchell, the b-17 Flying Fortress, the b-50 Super-fortress, the b-47 Stratojet, and the b-29 Superfortress. This is the history of the Hurricane Hunters. These are the planes that have carried the men and the women into storms. But at least one plane is missing: the two-seat AT-6. As legend has it, in 1943 a group of pilots in Bryan, Texas, was talking about moving their planes away from an approaching storm. Some of the pilots said the AT-6s couldn't stand the weather. But Lt. Col. Joe Duckworth, for whatever reason, said the AT-6 could fly in anything. One of the other pilots dared him to prove it, and so Duckworth did. With Ralph O'Hair, a navigator on base, he entered the storm somewhere between 5,000 and 6,000 feet over the roiling ocean. They made their way to the eye, more by accident and grace than anything like planning, and then returned to their base. Duckworth convinced the base weather officer to ride on another flight straightaway, and, as the story goes, the Hurricane Hunters got their start. On August 7, 1944, the War Department created the Third Weather Reconnaissance Squadron.

* * *

Four o'clock in the morning, and the crew has gathered in the meeting room for the preflight mission briefing. Models of airplanes and helicopters hang from the ceiling. Crew members sit widely spaced apart, and I find myself wondering if they are savoring their last bit of room before a very long day.

The officer in charge of the briefing, Maj. Gordon Ford, stands behind a podium on the stage, two large projection screens behind him. He goes over the mission objectives and procedures in front of screens that say Mission Set-up, and then Tasking.

"Scheduled departure time is six local, adjusted as necessary," he says. "The primary aircraft is 866 on spot 20. It *is* sealed, and they did just break the seal to pump you guys up to max gas. Your spare aircraft is 94 on spot 11 . . ." He goes on to describe the state of the plane we will fly, basic checklist stuff, procedures, and the crew nods—nothing surprising yet. At some point he mentions that our altitude in the storm will be 10,000 feet. When he calls on the weather officer, though, the mood of the room changes fast. This is the variable stuff. This is off the checklist.

A young woman in the row in front of me speaks up, 2nd Lt. Eileen Govan. What she says sounds like code. "Yes, sir. At 21z the forecast coordinates were 19.0 north, 81.4 west, and it's moving 290 at 8 knots. It's undergoing some quote-unquote weakening and strengthening. The other thing is that it's going through an eye-wall replacement cycle. The eye wall pressure is like 910 . . ."

Someone behind me lets out a long, soft whistle.

". . . and it's 161 knots. But on the latest pass they got 140 in the northeast. We've got a lot of planes out there with us. NOAA four-nine will be taking off at 17:30z. They'll be up at 40. And then we've got two P3s. NOAA four-three taking off at 9z. They'll be at 8,000 until NOAA four-two gets out there. They're taking off at 14z and then they'll be at 7, and four-three will go up to 12. And that's about all that I have for you right now."

Moving 290 at 8 knots, I think. As in 290 degrees on a 360-degree circle. It's moving just slightly north of straight west. Eight knots is not quite 10 miles an hour. Winds of 161 knots means 185 miles an hour. And the pressure is only 910 millibars (mb). The lower the pressure, the stronger the storm. Hurricane Andrew, the most expensive storm to hit the United States, was weaker at 922 mb. Hurricane Camille, often called the worst storm to ever hit the mainland United States, was 909 mb.

A man in the front row speaks up. Maj. Dallas Englehart, the aircraft pilot and commander. "What's four-nine going to be at?" In addition to our plane, and the J model behind us, there are going to be three other planes from the National Oceanic and Atmospheric Association (NOAA) in the same storm at the same time. NOAA four-nine will be above the storm. NOAA four-three and NOAA four-two will be close enough to pass coffee.

"Four-nine's going to be at 40." She says, "Once we get out there we'll probably need to start talking to them."

Someone in the room chuckles. Another one says, "Yeah . . ."

This is a very strong storm. Hurricane-force winds exist from the eye outward about 90 miles. Tropical storm–force winds blow 200 miles out. And it's going to be crowded, too.

* * *

In truth, there are two organizations that claim the Hurricane Hunters name. The first, and the oldest, is the Fifty-third. But NOAA has its own fleet of aircraft based at MacDill Air Force Base outside Tampa, Florida, and its own slightly different mission. They fly the Gulfstream IV special-performance jet, NOAA 49, above the hurricane at 40,000-plus feet to measure the steering winds that push the storm one way or another. And they fly two WP-3D Orions, research aircraft used to study storms and the atmosphere all over the world. Although the missions and the data do overlap a bit, Lori Bast, a public affairs specialist with the NOAA Aircraft Operations Center, once told me there was an easy way to understand the difference. The air force, she said, is doing reconnaissance. They want to know where the storm is going. NOAA, she said, is looking at the storm itself. They want to know what the storm is doing, and why.

* * *

The briefing continues, back to the checklists. There is talk about emergency procedures. Englehart looks around the room. "How many do we have on board today? It looks like . . ." He pauses. "A bunch." Everyone laughs. "We'll get a good count later," he says. And then there is talk about fuel-transfer rates. At some point, Major Ford mentions that we will be doing something unique. As far as he knows, he says, this is the first time a Hurricane Hunter flight has been cleared to fly over Cuba on the way to and back from the storm. Cuba, I think? We're flying over Cuba? As a matter of courtesy, Ford tells us, we've been asked to turn off our cameras when we are in Cuban airspace.

We are dismissed, and another crew files into the briefing room. Another C-130 will be with us in the storm today. This is one of the newer J-model planes, with stronger engines and what's called a glass cockpit—digital displays for the flight instruments instead of the now old-fashioned gauges, though a few of those are still included as reliable backups. They are doing radar testing, we're told. No reporters will be on that plane, though. As we linger in the lobby in front of the mural, I notice there is a lighted sign above the doorway to the briefing room, much like the on-air light at radio or TV stations. This one reads "Classified." It goes on for a while, then goes off. Then it goes on again. Then it goes off.

Crew members cross the lobby on their way from one thing to another, and often joke as they pass. "What's our altitude to-day?" one asks. "Ten thousand," is the reply. "And NOAA is going to be where?" the first person asks. "Ten thousand one hundred."

Major Englehart, the pilot, stops to say it's three hours and fifteen minutes from takeoff to the center of the eye, and we need to leave right on time. He says the eye right now is very well formed. We should be able to see quite a lot. And we should have an interesting ride to get there. Englehart is a pilot for Northwest Airlines. He flies in and out of Alaska a lot, and he's been to my home airport, Hector Field in Fargo, North Dakota, many times. Another crew member is a DC-10 pilot. On the crew's flight suits there are patches for their names, for the flag of the United States, for the Hurricane Hunters, and for the Reserve. Oftentimes, the patches for the Reserve are topped by a number, the number of logged hours a person has flown in uniform. The lowest number I see is 2,000. On one man's uniform there is a patch that reads "Graduate Air Force Test Pilot School."

A crew member, short, hair cut to nearly bald, bright smile and easy laugh, talks to Eaton for a while and then gathers the CNN crew, Chelsea and Tom, and me into the coffee room with the round table. This is the briefing for media.

"Good morning," he says. "I'm Staff Sergeant Scherzer. You've met Airman Eaton, who is your PA rep. We're pretty much going to be your coordination for most of the day in the back of the airplane. Most of the crew is primarily up front, and you'll see that when we go out. The two pilots, navigator, weather officer, and a flight engineer all sit up front of the dropsonde console, where I sit. The dropsonde operator is all the way in the rear of the cargo portion of the airplane. So we'll be in the back. Anyway, the main thing for you guys today is emergency. *If* we have an actual emergency, we'll give you a heads-up to get seated, and we might just use the hand signals to just buckle up. It's a real old, loud airplane. It's probably not anything you've ever experienced if you haven't been on a military aircraft. Has anyone flown on a C-130 before?"

Not one hand goes up.

"So. It's just a real old, real loud plane. You really can't hear a lot when you're speaking. Off headset, just try to really speak up and project your voice. It's not being rude, it's just you can't hear otherwise. You know people are sometimes polite."

Scherzer goes over the procedure for getting on and off the headset communications within the plane. He explains that when he's talking to us, he is also listening to the flight crew.

"The main thing for me is when we get into the storm environment. When we're about 20 to 30 miles out from the eye wall, we'll probably start seeing a little moderate turbulence. And then severe to extreme turbulence within that three-, four-, five-minute time frame from eye wall to clearing the eye to the eye wall again. So everybody's pretty much going to be buckled up."

Scherzer brings his arms and hands around and gives the hand signal for buckling a seat belt.

"We'll talk to the aircraft commander whether or not we're going to do any circling or things in the eye. But it's usually a straight shot across the eye. So we will have a few minutes when you're able to jump out of your seat, grab a couple pictures out the scanner windows of the eye wall. So today being a day flight, it looks pretty clear right now, what I was looking at on radar, so it should be pretty dramatic. Stadium effect, we call it, with the clouds built all around us and stuff. So that'll be cool. We'll give you a heads-up, a thumbs-up . . ."—he brings his arms around again, this time two thumbs up—"that you can get up and grab a couple of pictures, and then I'll say sit back down when we're about thirty to forty-five seconds of penetrating the eye wall again."

Englehart stops in the coffee room. Govan stops in too. Both of them give or check some information with Scherzer.

"I do have life vests out," he says to us again. "When we get on the airplane you'll see green and yellow life vests. Sit where there is a yellow one. Those are designated for passengers. It's right in the center of the airplane, in the wheel well of the airplane, is where I have you guys sitting today. The main thing, if you're feeling sick, queasy, I have plenty of water, as Mike was saying earlier. He sees it a lot, people not used to being bounced around and having a good stomach. If you like roller coasters, you'll like the ride today; if you get queasy, we do have little yellow bags for your disposal, and up front we do have a Porta Potty, a commercial-style aircraft bathroom if you need to go in there. Or there is a large garbage can to do your business."

All of us at the table laugh at this, albeit nervously.

"Those are your friends today," he says, smiling hugely. I imagine the crew loves it when civilians can't take the ride. "The Porta Potty and the garbage can. The aircraft rule is 'You mess it up, you clean it up.' There'll be nobody babysitting you today in that regard. Anyone have any questions for me?"

We ask about electrical outlets for laptop computers, about what windows we should use. The directions are easy.

"All right, I'm going to finish this paperwork," he says. "We have about another ten minutes now if you want to start asking other questions or get down to the shop, now would be the time to do that. Use the restroom, get all the last-minute things done. Have a good time."

Moderate, severe, extreme turbulence, I think. Our life vests are somehow not the same as the crew's, I think. "Have a good time," he said. I try to find some apprehension in my breath, thinking there should be some. But all I feel is wonderfully excited.

* * *

At 5:30 in the morning, we walk under the sign ("Through these doors . . .") and outside to the tarmac. Some part of me hopes the plane will be right there. Some part of me hopes for a send-off, perhaps just a little drum and bugle corps. But all that waits is a pair of white vans and, in a car a short distance away, military police to make sure we don't wander off. We pack into the vans and are driven to the airplane.

The c-130 is a large plane, gunmetal gray with a black nose, high wings, and a very high tail to allow for the ramp at the back of the fuselage. The wingspan is 132 feet, 7 inches. The top of the tail is 38 feet, 3 inches above the ground. The whole thing is 97 feet, 9 inches long. There are a lot of large windows for the personnel on the flight deck, one large observation window on each side a bit farther back, and then just porthole-size glass once or twice more. There is nothing about it that says sleek or fast or sexy. This is the Jeep of the air force. It goes anywhere and hauls just about anything. The h model, which is our plane, has two Allison turboprop engines, each rated at 4,300 horsepower, hanging from each wing. Four blades per propeller. The newer j model looks nearly identical to the h, but from the wings hang four Rolls-Royce engines, each rated at 4,700 horsepower. Each propeller on the j model has six blades. The w before c-130 of either model means, simply, "weather."

The cnn pair stops to record the moment. Blake films Bellini, who hypes the danger. Then Tom films Chelsea, who talks about the pressure readings and wind speeds. We board the airplane and find a place for our camera bags. One by one then, the engines start.

The plane needs to be pushed back a bit, and the tail ramp is lowered and crew members stand on the ramp, ready to signal if there's an obstruction. But there is nothing in the way, and we don't need to back up very far, so at 5:45 in the morning the ramp is raised and the inside of the plane turns aquamarine. In the tactical versions of this plane, the center of the fuselage is where Jeeps would be parked, or where dozens of paratroopers would get ready for their dive into the sky, or where cargo would be lashed to pallets and then either unloaded on the ground or dropped from the air. But in the weather version, the hold is essentially one giant tank, 11,000 pounds, of aviation gasoline. There is what Sergeant Scherzer called a Porta Potty, complete with crescent moon painted on the door. And one long bench runs the left side of the cabin for us to sit on. Red canvas webbing is our back support. Bunks for resting crew members are tucked in corners over our heads. The dropsonde station, where Scherzer sits, is behind the gas tank and just in front of the ramp.

We all have earplugs in, but the plane is still very loud. Scherzer tells the CNN crew to strap their bags into the seats. He doesn't want any loose bags on this flight. The plane begins to taxi, but with no windows I cannot tell where we are.

There is a pause, and then the brakes are released and the engines go to full power. I look at my watch and wait to feel the rotation of nose wheels into air. It's 6:20 in the morning, and we are airborne. We are flying toward Hurricane Ivan.

* * *

The sun rises over the Gulf of Mexico and through the few windows we can see oil platforms down in the still-smooth water. Thunderheads cloud the sky, backlit by the sun, turning orange and blue and yellow and red. It is a brilliant and gorgeous morning out there. Dramatic, too, with the way every cloud seems to hint toward the clouds we're chasing. One layer of clouds, fairly low, is joined by another layer higher up. Building.

At the dropsonde station, Sergeant Scherzer checks his equipment. Airman Eaton begins to escort us media types to the flight deck to interview the crew. First goes CNN. Then Chelsea and Tom. When it's my turn, I'm led up the small stairwell and given a headset. It takes some time to get the connections right. Outside the windows I see a summer's day, slightly cloudy. You wouldn't think there was anything special anywhere near. In the headset, I can hear air traffic control as well as the flight crew.

Englehart, the pilot, is the first voice in my ears. ". . . we'll put on 40 Yankee, 'cause they're going to be on 92 or so."

"What are you putting it on?" someone asks.

The navigator responds. "29. It should be 29 Yankee 92."

"If we're talking about for the J guys, they want us to go to 30 Yankee."

"Yeah, 30 Yankee, oh, okay."

"Did I say something different?"

"I didn't know what you said."

"Okay, yeah. That's fine."

I have no idea what they are talking about.

Englehart asks the copilot, "Did you guys have this, or did you have one of those skins things?"

"Skins" is really scns, I know. The self-contained navigation system.

"I had one of those way back when at some point, yeah," he says.

"You flew skins, right? You guys were skins over in Minnesota, weren't you?"

The Minnesota Air Guard is made up of two wings. The 148th Fighter Wing is based in Duluth, and they fly f-16s. What everyone sees, however, when they fly commercial jets in or out of Minneapolis–St. Paul, is the 133rd Airlift Wing. They fly the c-130. But listening to the crew, it occurs to me only now that these guys don't know each other. They may have flown thousands of hours, and we are heading toward a hurricane, but they have not flown those hours together.

Another voice pipes in. "On the hour, sir, crews changing. 150.3 on the gross weight."

"Thanks," Englehart says.

"Let's skew a little more to the left here," someone says.

Air traffic control calls, "Continental 1891 contact Houston Center 132.17. Good day."

The Continental flight calls back, "132.17 Continental 1891. See you later."

The controller and the Continental pilot both sound happy, like they are having real fun.

Finally, my headset is connected right, and I turn to Eileen Govan, the weather officer. Young, late twenties maybe, brown hair pulled into a bun on the back of her head, her seat is farthest back on the flight deck. What I really want to do is just watch her work, just watch all of these people and listen closely. Flying is something you *do*. But I have the chance to ask questions.

"Tell me what you do at this station?" I ask.

"Well," she says, a southern accent hiding in her voice, "I'm the meteorologist. I'm collecting all the data here."

"And that gets sent in real time back to the Hurricane Center?"

"Yes. When we get to 105 nautical miles from the storm, I turn on a high-density observation system. And it puts a report together. Every one minute that information is compiled and sent to the Hurricane Center."

"Do you do any computer modeling here on the plane, or is that all back there?"

"No. The Hurricane Center does everything of that nature. We don't forecast; we're just reconnaissance."

"Okay," I say. "How many flights have you been on? I was looking for a number above your badge there for flight hours."

Govan smiles broadly, like she's a bit embarrassed, or like a secret's been let out.

"Oh," she says, "I'm still in training. This is my first year. Right now, I think this is my ninth flight, if I'm not mistaken."

"And what's it like for you after nine flights?"

"It's, ah," she pauses. "I'm getting used to it."

"You're not quite used to it yet?"

"I'm pretty well," she says, looking away and out the cockpit window. "I'm getting it down." She sounds confident, I think.

"Tell me about your first flight?" I ask.

"My first flight. It was in Hurricane Alex. We deployed out of Florida, and I was extremely excited. It was just at the formation stages. So it wasn't nearly like what today is gonna be."

"Today's going to be a bit of a ride?"

The voice of the navigator breaks into the headset, talking to the pilot.

"Come back to the right a little bit. You got this line now, basically you'll be parallel. You can come back right about a couple of degrees. Twenty degrees and just parallel."

There are already storms outside. Bands of thunderstorms that rotate out and away from the hurricane's center. We are still a long way away, but the signs are starting. Govan turns and does a quick visual scan of her equipment.

"Did you go into the air force to do meteorology or meteorology and then the air force?" I ask. "How did those two come together for you?"

Govan smiles and laughs a bit. "Actually, I went to the University of South Alabama, Mobile, and I majored in meteorology. And this just kind of happened." Her eyes widen with her smile at the happenstance of it all.

"Hurricane Hunters always been a dream of yours?"

"I've always been interested in it; I never really saw myself doing it. There's only twenty-three of us, you know, in this career field. It's pretty unique. So, absolutely I was interested, but I never thought it would actually work out like it did."

"It's got to be a thrill to do this," I say.

Govan's laugh fills the back of the flight deck. "For a meteorologist, it is great."

We move on to the more technical side of her job. "Tell me what kind of data you do collect," I say. "I know wind speed and air pressure and those kind of things. What else is collected here by the things that you drop and by the instruments on board?"

Govan's demeanor turns professional. Now she's giving the standard media tour.

"Let's see," she says. "Pretty well we do temperature, dew point, the radar altitude, pressure altitude, wind direction, wind speed, and there's a system, you may want to talk to the navigator about, it's called a skin. It's a self-contained navigation system. They also do wind speed as well as the latitude, longitude, everything we use to fix the storm."

"How many fixes do you get during a flight like this?"

"It depends. On a normal flight we do four fixes. So we penetrate the storm four times."

"And of all the readings you take, is that the most important? The pressure in the eye?"

"That is what they're looking for back in the Hurricane Center. In between the four fixes, we get a trend and we get a movement, and they're very interested in that."

"What is the pressure right now, in the eye?"

"Right now, they just fixed it at 919, so it's going up just a little bit. But it's kind of going through an eye-wall replacement cycle. So it's going to undergo some fluctuations, but they're expecting for it to settle back out."

"What would be a significant rise in pressure to signal that the storm is weakening?"

"Oh, my," she says. "It takes about an hour and forty-five minutes between fixes, and if you see anything around 10 millibars, that would be a pretty good jump. You kind of expect, if you think it's going to undergo some sort of cycle where it's going to be changing, you expect a millibar or 2 or 3. But 10 will let you know that something is really going on."

"And what do you expect when we get there today?"

"Hopefully, I expect something around 919, not too much more!"

"And what are the maximum winds right now?"

"Max winds that they've seen so far today was 161 knots."

Govan looks at me, wondering, I'm sure, if I know what she's just said about the combination of pressure and wind, about the fast dance this plane is about to attempt. I thank her for her time, and with a fast "No problem," we're done.

* * *

Outside the cockpit windows, the sky is still good. Partly cloudy, with beautiful thunderhead formations in the left and right distance. White clouds turning indigo and red. Looking out a low window, past the pilot's left leg, I can see the Gulf of Mexico smooth enough to reflect the clouds. So far, not a bump in the sky.

My next interview is with Lt. Col. Doug Rose, the navigator. But we don't get started right away. When we get the headset turned to his voice, I hear him talking with the pilot. Cuba is just ahead.

". . . we'll just be approaching their no-fly line. Does that make sense?"

"Yeah."

"You'll have enough gas if they don't let us fly over for some reason."

"Sure do."

"Okay, like if we have to go around or something."

"No sweat."

"You got that kind of gas. We're planning on that. Plan for the worst."

Rose gets out of his seat to look over the pilot's shoulder, then sits back down and looks at me. He turns and picks up a chart of the Gulf, puts it on his leg, and holds it up as a prop for my video camera, then turns back to me. He's done this before. Not very long ago, surfing through channels on the television, I found a hurricane show on the Discovery Channel. There was Lt. Col. Doug Rose seated in the navigator's seat, holding a chart, talking to a camera.

"Good morning," I say.

"Good morning," he says.

"You're the navigator," I say.

And we're off. The lecture begins.

"That's right. This mission here I'm navigating us down. Currently, we're in the middle of the Gulf of Mexico, and we're headed down to the western tip of Cuba. We will fly over Cuba. We have diplomatic clearance to do that. This will be the first time this year actually that we've been able to fly over Cuba. Years previous we have not had that coordination done. So this is quite an improvement in the relationships at least between the Hurricane Hunters and Cuba."

I force an interruption. "Do you think that's because of the storm, or is there something else in Washington that's made that possible?"

"No, it's primarily because of the storms and the fact that they are affected severely by these storms as well, and they have, since the last year, felt it reasonable to allow us to fly over. So, a big improvement. And I can't really talk about the negotiations, because I wasn't part of that. However," he continues, "as we fly over the western coast of Cuba, we will be headed down toward the Grand Caymans. The storm currently is predicted to be just south, slightly southwest of the Grand Cayman Island here, and it will be proceeding just slightly to the west unless we find the center to be different, and it could very easily in fact fly right over the Grand Caymans. Current winds as was mentioned by the weather officer approximately 165 miles per hour, sustained, so we can expect gusts around the Grand Caymans of something greater than that. We're looking at the weather bands extending out approximately 75 to 100 miles, and so therefore as we pass over Cuba you should start seeing the weather become bad. We'll have some weather at the altitude here just prior to us descending. We'll descend down to 10,000 feet just prior to entering our first leg. We'll proceed into the hurricane at 10,000 feet, and you should have quite a bit of heavy weather at that point. We'll see a lot of turbulence, a lot of thunderstorms. I'll be doing some deviations. However, I can't deviate freely because we need to get good data to be able to translate this information to NOAA, so they can make a good determination on the movement of this storm. So when we get closer to the eye wall, my opportunities to deviate from the track are lessened, and we will probably be going through some pretty severe weather bands. That's what I expect."

I almost start laughing. Rose knows I want stories of high weather, of terror in the sky, of drama and excitement, and those are the details he's offering without my asking. His deviations, his paths around storms to keep us safe, might not be possible. We might have to fly right into the heart of the thing. We need good data. Pretty severe weather bands be damned.

"The location and strength of the thunderstorm cells," I ask, "are those important for the hurricane track, or is that just a by-product of the storm itself?"

"It's a by-product of the storm. And the cells which are embedded primarily in the eye wall and the feeder bands, unfortunately, they're not really trackable. It's the eye wall and the center of the hurricane that we're looking to track. Now," he continues, "one of the major considerations that I have as a navigator is, as we fly through the storms and cells of feeder bands and the eye wall, there are embedded tornadoes, and these embedded tornadoes are particularly dangerous to us because there you're experiencing winds in excess of 200 knots, and that could be disastrous to this aircraft. So we make sure that we avoid those particular items. It's a tough job to get through the eye wall. You'll notice that as we go through."

"How fast have you seen tornadoes form in front of an airplane?" I ask.

"Normally, because the entire eye wall is moving at 70 knots to 100 knots, it's a little hard to actually track them. In fact, I'll be so busy, I'll be just looking to avoid them. I don't really care once they're behind me where they're going."

"But you can see them forming fast enough to get the plane around them most of the time?"

"Yes, that's correct." He pauses and then smiles. "We shall hope so."

"With the equipment you've got on board, do you generally get a good 3-D picture of the storm?"

"Well, it's a two-dimensional picture that I get on my plane scope here, my PPI." He points to a plan position indicator, the most common type of radar screen. Round with a sweeping line, the airplane in the middle. "But I get quite a good representation of the storm, much better than the weather officer who's looking at pressure, winds. She doesn't have quite the visual that I have, so I'm the one that'll direct us into the point where we're proceeding into the eye wall, in which case I'll give her one last heading to what I determine to be the center visually. And then she'll take over and start to determine off her instruments where the minimum pressure and the minimum winds, probably zero zero on the winds that we should call the center."

Zero zero is wind from zero direction on a compass at zero speed. Dead calm.

A woman's voice comes into the headset. "Houston Center, NOAA 49 . . ." One of the other Hurricane Hunters is calling in. The rest of the conversation is lost to me, though.

"Be advised," Rose says, "that's the center at altitude, 10,000 feet. It may not be exactly the center on the surface. As we proceed out through the storm we'll go out on the other side and take it out about 105 miles, 105 nautical miles, so we will go through the eye wall twice on every pass. We will experience the eye itself on every pass as well."

All I do is nod.

"Due to the strength of this particular storm," he goes on, "we will be experiencing drift of approximately 45 to 55 degrees of drift. That much drift will actually make our forward movement approximately 40–50 percent of what it normally is. It extends our time in the eye wall, it gives us a chance to experience more of the eye wall's . . . ," he pauses, "unique experiences."

We both laugh at this. There is no language, it seems, for the experience of flying through the eye wall of a hurricane. And this is a very big hurricane. The drift, however, is something I understand. Imagine a plane that is trying to fly north, but there is a strong crosswind from the west. To correct for the push toward the east, the pilot points the plane slightly into the wind. It's called crabbing into the wind. When Rose tells me there will be 45 to 55 degrees of drift, what he's really telling me is that the plane will be pointed 45 to 55 degrees off the direction it's actually traveling.

"You should also sense a great deal of temperature change as we proceed into the eye," Rose says. "You will actually descend in the eye wall because we're maintaining a constant 10,000-foot indicated, so we've got to descend down into the lower pressures of the eye wall. So as we do you will sense great, ah, significant temperature increase, even with the air conditioners we have on the aircraft."

In other words, I think, to maintain an indicated 10,000 feet of altitude in the tremendous uprush of air in the eye wall, we will be pointed down. We will be 45 to 55 degrees off center and pointed down, just to maintain level flight and hold a course. This should be fun.

"How many times through the eye do you think we'll go today?" I ask.

"We'll go four times, that's for certain. Unless something happens to the aircraft, we expect four times. It could be five. Sometimes we're asked to extend. Currently, today, we're looking right on the edge of a fifth pass. Probably not, but if it was absolutely necessary for prediction, we might entertain that."

"Okay. Thank you very much," I say. "I'm looking forward to it."

"Very good. And you're welcome. I'm looking forward to it as well. It's always a challenge."

* * *

Although we are still a good distance away, the airplane approaches the north shore of Cuba. Airman Eaton reminds us all that we're not allowed to take pictures in Cuban airspace. There's nothing we could take, no picture with our commonplace 35mm and TV cameras that would reveal any secret, but this is a courtesy that's been asked for in return for crossing the airspace. No one mentions it, but I'm sure everyone on board remembers the two planes from the Brothers to the Rescue organization shot down by Cuban MIGs in February 1996. Brothers to the Rescue is a group of Cuban exiles that flies the space between Florida and Cuba looking for rafts, small boats, anyone trying to make the journey north. Cuba said the planes were in their airspace. A pilot in a third plane said they were not. Looking out the flight deck windows, I wonder about the other WC-130, the J model, behind us. And I wonder about the three planes from NOAA. All of us are crossing Cuba this morning.

I have one more interview on the flight desk. Major Englehart is the pilot for this flight. And if Eaton is the strong and silent type, Scherzer the funny guy, Govan the wide-eyed new kid on the plane, and Rose the been-there-done-that guy, then Englehart is the movie star. Hollywood handsome with blond hair, he'd look good in a leather jacket and long white scarf.

This is the guy I want to pick apart, and I have no idea what to ask. The plane is in his hands when the weather hits. He feels in his hands and arms and feet and legs the shake of the whole thing. When the nose goes down, it's his hands that pull back on the yoke. When we're 45 degrees off center and pointed down in an eye wall, it's his brain that needs to say this makes sense. Just like Duckworth in the AT-6, this is the guy who *flies* in the storm. All I really want to ask is only *What is it like?* But I already know there is no way to answer that question. It's a stupid question to even try. What would he say other than "Damn scary" or "It's like wow"? So I ask the mundane questions, hoping to dance around the deeper stuff and maybe see it that way. I start by asking how many times he's done this before. Probably fifteen storms, he says. Four to five penetrations of the eye on each flight, and sometimes more than one flight per storm. So somewhere near one hundred times in one side of the eye of a hurricane and then out the other.

"Other than keeping the plane stable," I ask, "what are the unique challenges flying through a hurricane?"

"Most of it's, like you said, keeping the plane stable," he says, and pauses. "Keeping the plane stable and trying to figure out where the eye is and fixing it, and coordinating with the whole crew, because it's a crew effort. The weather officer, the navigator, the dropsonde operator, engineer also. Just coordinate with everybody, keep everybody in the loop, and try to fix the storm so the National Hurricane Center gets good information so we can track this storm and see where it's going to hit landfall. Hopefully, it never does hit landfall, but more than likely the ones we're on are going to hit landfall. That's why they want us to go out there and see them."

"Is the c-130 a relatively forgiving, easy plane to fly, then, in a situation like this, or is it a real struggle?"

"Well, at moments it's a struggle," he says. "It depends on how bad the storm is and how bad the turbulence is. It depends if you have any maintenance challenges like . . ." He pauses. "I've shut down engines before in storms, and it's just real challenging as far as that. As far as a good airplane, it's been around for going on about fifty years, so it's obviously a forgiving airplane and obviously the air force likes it because they're going to the new J models. So, yeah, I would say it's a pretty forgiving airplane."

"I heard that as we get close to the eye wall we get some ice, get some hail, that kind of stuff. What other conditions do you think we're going to fly through, or we might fly through, that would be a particular challenge from the piloting standpoint?"

"Well, I mean, obviously, the turbulence, severe turbulence, anywhere from moderate to severe. So, I mean, we can get bounced around pretty good. Obviously, there's lightning involved, and hail. Everybody in this crew's been struck by lightning at least once or twice. So, there's a lot of weather—I mean, obviously, it's a huge weather phenomenon. There's a lot of weather stuff involved there."

"Weather stuff," I think. Got it. Is there any good way to describe the ride we're on? I remember reading someone's description of a stunt pilot as carving a line in the sky, as a kind of art. But the stunt pilot does the tricks on purpose. The stunt pilot chooses what trick, and when. The stunt pilot does not worry about tornadoes embedded in bands of thunderstorms embedded in the eye wall of a category 5 hurricane over the open and violent ocean. No one on the ground will applaud when Englehart flies his plane. But when we land, we will owe him our lives.

"Are there a lot of pilots who want to take your seat someday?"

"We usually have new people—in fact, we've got a bunch of new lieutenants in here—so yeah, I think people find it an exciting mission. Something different, something challenging. So, yeah, we usually get a lot of applications to come fly with the Hurricane Hunters."

"This strikes me as a real prestige position."

"I don't know about that," he says modestly. The other crew members, listening to our conversation, laugh into their headsets.

"I'm trying to get the others guys to laugh here," I tell Englehart.

"You still got to buy your own drinks at the club, don't'cha now?" the copilot asks, a thick southern accent in my ears.

"What's that? I got you punched off," Englehart asks him.

"I said you still gotta buy your own drinks at the club."

Englehart smiles and I am about to ask another question, but there is this island approaching and I am told it's time to leave the flight deck.

* * *

Back in the main part of the C-130, I see Chelsea and Tom finishing up an interview with Scherzer at the dropsonde station. I assume the CNN crew has gone first there too; the two men sit on the long bench, their backs against the red webbing. We still have a few moments until Cuba, some more time until the storm itself, so I hustle to the back of the plane myself, to learn what goes on there. Passing the scan windows, I look outside. Still a sunny sky. Still a beautiful day.

Scherzer hands me a headset, and once again I can hear all the conversations in the plane.

"Good morning, again," I say.

"Good morning."

"I promise to ask you the same questions you've been asked by everyone else in your career," I tell him.

Scherzer smiles at me.

"Can you tell me a little bit about this station and the kind of work that's done back here?" I ask.

"Sure," he says. "My job is the . . ."

A voice in my headset interrupts us. It's not Englehart, but it's certainly someone from the flight deck. I don't know who it is.

"I *think* she said 'permission granted,'" he says.

There is a pause. "It doesn't hurt to say 'Muchas gracias' or something," Englehart replies.

"I'm hearing the flight crew," I tell Scherzer.

"Yeah, you want me to take that off?" he asks.

View from the runway at Grise Fiord looking south over possible explorer graves and then Jones Sound. Photo by author.

Above: Steve Kaizer *(left)* and Rory MacNicol *(right)* in front of Twin Otter C-GPAO. Photo by author.

Top Right: Twin Otters with skis outside a Polar Continental Shelf Project building. Photo by author.

Bottom Right: Steve Kaizer bringing C-GPAO out in the morning. Photo by author.

Above: Looking for the expedition at 87 degrees north. Tough place to land. Photo by Stephen Kaizer.

Right: Found! The expedition at 87 degrees north getting ready for a supply drop. Photo by Stephen Kaizer.

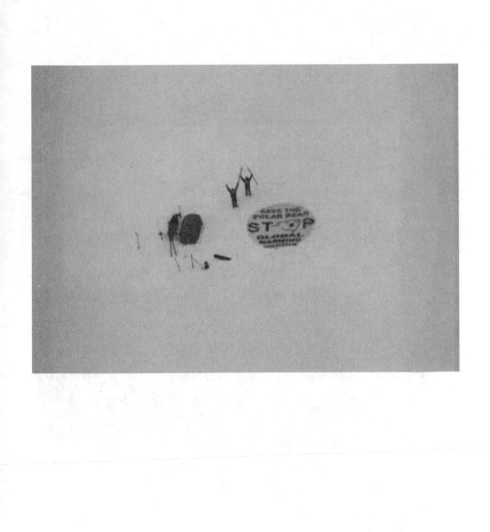

Left: Rescuing the dog team. Photo by Stephen
Kaizer.

Above: Tight quarters, but safe. Photo by
Stephen Kaizer.

Left: Loading the dogs—not a place to linger.
Photo by Stephen Kaizer.

Above: Sleds against the wall, dogs in the
middle. Everyone comfortable? Photo by
Stephen Kaizer.

Above: One end of the runway at Grise Fiord.
Photo by author.

Right: The other end of the runway at Grise
Fiord. Note go-around path through hills to
left. Photo by author.

Above: The Narwhal Hotel. Photo by author.

Right: Dan Minsky. Photo by Ranjit Sangra.

Top Left: Sign over the doorway to the
airplanes at Keesler Air Force Base. Photo by
author.

Bottom Left: A c 130 equipped for the Fifty-
third Weather Reconnaissance Squadron—the
Hurricane Hunters. Photo by author.

Above: Four o'clock in the morning, the
briefing for the day's flight to Hurricane Ivan.
Photo by author.

Above: Clouds over the Caribbean on the way
to Ivan. Photo by author.

Right: Clouds inside Ivan. Photo by author.

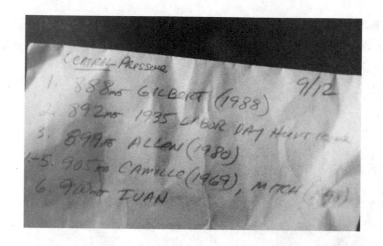

Top Left: A note passed during the ride in the storm. At the time, Ivan was the sixth-strongest Hurricane on record. Photo by author.

Bottom Left: Maj. Dallas Englehart, the aircraft pilot and commander. Photo by author.

Above: The dropsonde station in the back of the C-130. Photo by author.

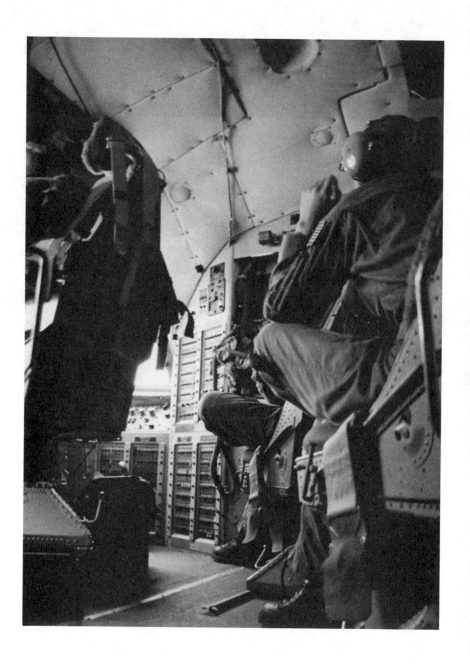

Left: View coming up the stairs to the flight deck. Weather officer and navigator to the right. Photo by author.

Above: Have a nice flight. Photo by author.

Top Left: MeritCare's Bell 222 on scene in
eastern North Dakota with a traffic accident.
Photo by Dwayne Chevalier.

Bottom Left: On scene with a snowmobile
accident. Photo by Jason Keefler.

Above: Tim Vreeman, MeritCare lead pilot,
over the Minnesota prairie. Photo by author.

Above: Dan Ehlen, LifeFlight program
director. Photo by author.

Right: Bell 222 in the rooftop hangar at
MeritCare in Fargo, North Dakota. Photo by
author.

Above: Approaching the rooftop helicopter deck at MeritCare. Photo by author.

Right: The whole crew, fixed-wing and helicopter. Photo by Dave Samson.

Above: Tanker 10. Photo by author.

Top Right: Earl Dahl, Tanker 10 pilot. Photo
by author.

Bottom Right: View out the nose bubble
of Tanker 10 on the way to a fire. Photo by
Nathan Hall.

Above: Tanker 10 landing at the Billings, Montana, tanker base. Photo by author.

Right: Tanker 10, jets open, in a steep turn while a SEAT passes below. Photo by Nathan Hall.

Above: Tanker oo. Photo by author.

Right: SEAT 407 at the loading pit. Photo by author.

Top Left: In the pits, loading a SEAT. Photo by author.

Bottom Left: Allen Edmonds, state aviation manager. Photo by author.

Above: Through the haze, a view of a racing grass fire. Photo by Nathan Hall.

Scherzer asks Eaton to change the settings on a control panel for my headset.

"Is that what she said?" the first voice asks. "'Permission granted?'"

"I missed it," Englehart says.

Scherzer tells the flight deck that the headsets have been changed.

"We've got about ten minutes," he's told. "And then we're going to brief up."

"Roger that," he replies.

Scherzer and I settle down into our interview, but in the back of my mind I am still processing what I heard. We're about to fly over Cuba, and they *think* she, I assume some military air traffic controller, said 'permission granted'?

Scherzer begins to answer the question I asked earlier.

"I'm a dropsonde-systems operator. I take the vertical observation in the storm, working with the weather officer who's up front taking the flight-level data at the same time. In the storm environment as we fly into the eye walls and the eye of the storm is where we drop the sondes, the dropsondes. These are instruments that fall 2,500 feet per minute collecting data as it falls every half second, getting the pressure, temperature, dew point, and wind direction and wind speed based on a GPS wind-finding card." Scherzer holds up a dropsonde, a tube that's sixteen inches long and a little more than two inches wide. It looks a bit like the tube in the middle of a roll of paper towels.

Englehart's voice interrupts again, ". . . pretty much shut that one off."

"So," Scherzer continues, "that becomes significant in the forecasting of the storm. Just to be able to find out what those significant winds are, and also the pressure inside the center of the storm to be able to determine . . ."

The second voice from the flight deck comes on. "Sounds like that worked out pretty good there. The first check-in."

Rose's voice joins in. "That worked just fine. She's, uh, quite a girl."

Scherzer gets up to adjust the headset-control panel. I can hear only him now, but he can't hear me. Then more adjustments and a conversation with the flight deck about who should be able to hear whom if what button is pushed in and what other button is pulled out. Finally, we're good to go.

"How many sondes do you drop in a storm?" I ask.

"Typically, four or five passes through the storm, dropping one in each eye wall and the center drop. So today would be twelve to fifteen sondes released in the storm environment. If we mark the center and the weather officer isn't happy with that or thought we might be off by a few miles and we're going to make another pass and turn around in the eye, sometimes that happens, to be able to get better, exact data. It's weather, so it's constantly changing, and the parameters are not always specific to each individual storm being individually different. That might happen a few times."

"What does a vertical picture tell us that a horizontal one doesn't?"

"It gives you a better picture from here to the sea surface. That is the main information that we're getting. We can't fly low enough to be able to understand exactly what is going on near the surface, so those winds and the pressure become significant at the surface of the storm because that's where it's going to be making landfall essentially, where the strongest winds are, what the pressure is there. The airplane does a great job of extrapolating data."

"Do they survive the splash in the ocean?" I ask.

"As soon as it hits the surface, the data will go to 9s. I know that the sonde's out of life; it's done. A one-time shot. It won't send data after it hits the surface. A kind of salinity disturbance. I don't remember the terminology, but the salinity of the ocean basically stops it from collecting data, so it won't continue to do so."

I ask Scherzer to tell me what he sees on his computer monitors, how to understand the information coming back to the plane from the falling dropsondes. He points to four columns, four channels of information coming back, and starts to explain it to me, but once again the conversation from the flight deck takes over the headsets.

"2099's behind us," says the southern accent.

"I don't even think I'm getting into that one," Englehart replies.

"Our course is going to be 149 going down to the descent. It's 169 spot 5, and that's our descent . . . ," Rose offers.

"Who owns the airspace down here? After Havana?" Englehart asks.

"Who owns the airspace on the other side of Havana?" Rose asks.

"Yeah. Who's that? Is it Venezuela?"

"Oh, no, no. No, this is Cayman. Grand Cayman."

There is talk about cross-feeding fuel from the external tanks. Englehart confirms the fuel information, then says, "Okay, basically the biggest deal here is figuring out the radials just totally suck."

I smile at Scherzer. Radials are radio beams sent from the ground stations called VORs, and they are part of how an airplane navigates. Scherzer, for his part, is still trying to explain the dropsonde console to me.

"So as soon as we launch the sonde, then the lapsed time will start, and this data will be from outside the airplane versus inside. Right now I know I have a good sonde, and it's collecting what's called the PTH data, the pressure temperature humidity, and it's getting a good signal back to its receiver."

"See if they got something in the . . . Hand me that Caribbean stuff. I can look it up for you," says a voice from the cockpit.

"For Havana?" asks Englehart.

"No, from the other side there. For Cayman."

"So," Scherzer continues, "that's how we know we're ready to go. So I'll touch a little button on the computer electronically; it will send a signal to the gate in the launch tube and make the sonde go out of the airplane."

Scherzer tells the flight crew their voices keep cutting into the headsets. "I'll let you talk about the dropsonde, pilot," Scherzer says, smiling.

"Well," Englehart says, "you guys can do it off headset. We're going to talk. We're over Cuba."

"Roger that."

"I think you're starting to see the first storms out there associated with the hurricane," Rose says. "Sure a good visual on Cuba today, though," he says.

There is a pause.

"Do you speak any Spanish at all?" Rose asks someone.

"Me?" asks Englehart.

"Yeah."

"Yeah, I'm totally fluent in it. Didn't you know?"

"Oh, I thought you might be."

"No . . ."

* * *

Cuba is green, agricultural, and pretty in the summer sunlight. The green is off the north shore. You would not think we were so many worlds apart. Flying over Cuba looks very much like flying over the United States—the brown of roads, the green of fields, rows of crops, shelterbelts and small towns. Off the north shore, the sea changes from deep blue to aqua green closer to shore. On land, near the west coast, country roads wind through hills and forests. If you didn't know better, you'd think today would be a perfect day to stay outside, perhaps to linger at the beach.

The western end of Cuba does not take very long to fly over. Already the southern shores move under the airplane, and we are back over open sea. I expect to see tremendous breakers on the Cuban beaches, towering waves crashing ashore. But a crew member tells me the seas are only 5 to 10 feet at the moment. I ask him why they aren't any bigger, and he says we're just a bit too far north still. Tonight, he says, those shores will look very different.

Looking as much as I can to the south out the side window, or around to the front of the airplane, I'm beginning to see clouds that indicate the border of Ivan. It's only 8:30 in the morning, and nearly all the talk inside the WC-130 has gone quiet. All the homework has been done, I think. But the test is still coming.

At 8:45 the sea becomes significantly whitecapped. The clouds become much thicker. We've just been told that in ten to fifteen minutes we'll be asked to strap in because we'll be in the storm's outer bands. The crew is battening things down, making sure everything is secure. It's been a fine, clear, sunny day so far, and except for the noise of the engines, this is a smooth flight, as smooth as any commercial airliner. But all that's about to change. In ten minutes we're going to be in a category 5 hurricane.

When the first bit of turbulence hits the plane, right at 9:00 in the morning, everyone becomes a little bit lighter in their seats. It isn't much of a bump. But for just a moment the plane is forced down, and we rise against our seat belts. Like the opening notes of a bolero, the bump means more than its own volume or force. We all sit back, reach for our belts, and wait for the next one. The interior of the WC-130 darkens as we begin to fly into clouds, and the sun is no longer bright, no longer comforting.

How do you explain the feeling of turbulence? How do you explain our worry? We laugh and smile when a roller coaster throws us against a strap or a seat, and we look at fast airplanes and fighter jets with the same kind of lust and desire we have for all the dangerous things we've made and we control. If we can say *I made this*, I think, then we want to see how far we can push our own making. But storms don't care at all for the things we've made. Turbulence is evidence that what we've made is small. The best we hope for today is to break even, to be alive and in the same shape we were when we entered the storm. We might even win, if you think about the information we collect and transmit back to the shore. But we do not say an ant in a boxing ring wins if the boxer fails to step on it.

There is a part of me that keeps waiting for in-flight announcements. "Ladies and gentlemen, this is your captain from the flight deck. We're going to encounter some turbulence. Please return to your seats. Fasten your seat belts, return your tray tables to their full and upright position." But there is no announcement here. We're simply going into a storm. A great, big killer storm. Thunderstorms, tornadoes, wind shear. Hurricane.

The inside of the plane darkens more as the clouds outside the few windows grow thicker. The turbulence is just a little bit worse. Nothing extreme yet. Just more frequent dips and rises. There is a crew man stationed at one of the scan windows. In his hand he holds a chart that tells him how to estimate wind speed at sea level by looking at the waves and the plumes of spray being blown off the tops of whitecaps. Every now and then he gets up and goes quickly up the stairs to the flight deck to share his observations, and then he returns to his window.

We can feel the props pull the plane as we change directions. Finally, we are in the storm and heading for the eye.

* * *

Three days ago, the Associated Press (AP) reported that Hurricane Ivan killed twelve people in Grenada and damaged 90 percent of the nation's homes with winds stronger than 140 miles an hour. "We are terribly devastated. It's beyond imagination," Prime Minister Keith Mitchell said.

Two days ago, the AP reported that Ivan's death toll was up to twenty-three and that although the storm had been downgraded to a category 4 storm, with winds still in excess of 150 miles an hour, Jamaican officials were trying to evacuate coastal areas. In the States, people began leaving the Florida Keys, and people in New Orleans were heading out as well.

Today, I have no idea what's happening on the ground. Rose has told me Grand Cayman is right in the path, and Govan has told me that winds might be heading back up toward 160 miles an hour. Back to category 5, with what is described as catastrophic damage. Here in the WC-130, when Scherzer gives us the hand signal to buckle up, we all find a place on the long bench and cinch ourselves in fast. What we imagine is the ride that will find us pinned to the floor and then the ceiling. Occasionally, I hear the solid metallic click of the dropsonde being shot out the underside of the airplane. The terrible violence doesn't come, though. I imagine Rose looking into his scope and directing Englehart around and between the hard air.

Then the crew signals that we can get up for a minute. We are in the eye of the hurricane! At the scan window, the crew tells us all that the eye is very poorly formed this morning. Just a lot of clouds and not the dramatic clear-blue sky with thick, churning cloud walls at the sides, the stadium effect that's so well known. "The storm is changing," we're told. The pressure has gone up, and the storm might be weakening. But this could just be temporary. Storms are dynamic, ever changing.

The first fix is made.

Time: 0547 Zulu (10:47 AM local)

Latitude: 18°26′ N

Longitude: 80°25′ W

Central pressure: 915 mb

Max wind: 133 knots

We turn. On our next pass, we're going to be coming in from the northeast quadrant, which is traditionally the roughest.

Scherzer and Eaton give us the signal to buckle up again, and we head to our seats. The eye wall is straight ahead, and when we enter it, we hit a headwind so strong we all have trouble staying upright in our places. One of the CNN bags comes rolling up the bench to me. We've made our first pass through the eye of Hurricane Ivan.

* * *

At 11:00 in the morning, the turbulence gets significantly worse. The plane is jostled and then battered by the winds and the rain. The plane banks to the left, then banks to the right. We are pressed into our seats and then nearly lifted out of them. The roar of the four turboprop engines makes it impossible to hear anyone. We're all wearing earplugs anyway. There's nothing to see out the scan windows except the thick gray of the storm clouds, which occasionally darken to nearly indigo blue, yet the crew man stationed at the window braces himself both left and right and waits for the chance to see anything at all.

The crew does not look worried. Airman Eaton and Scherzer are reading magazines. Even though we're in the storm, we're too far away for the dropsondes to be useful. There's very little for the rest of us to do except sit against the netting, try to doze and relax. When we get closer, Scherzer sits up, and again I can hear the sound of a dropsonde being launched. Occasionally, the observation crew member will turn around, look the length of the fuselage to Scherzer, and they share something, some look. Even though I can't see out the window, I can feel the plane continue to bank to the right or bank to the left. I can hear the engines increase or decrease and imagine Englehart adding or scaling back on the throttle. It's a wild ride.

Much brighter sunshine comes through the windows suddenly. After a good bit of turbulence to get in here, the ride is smooth again. We all unbuckle, grab our cameras, and race to the windows. The eye is still a jumbled mess of clouds. Once in it, however, we can see the terrible seas down below. Whitecaps with plumes that trail away like storm clouds over Everest. Huge waves. When these waves hit shore, they will turn into a storm surge and destroy homes and businesses and hospitals. These waves will carry people back out to sea.

The second fix is made.

Time: 0729 Zulu (12:29 PM local time)

Latitude: 18°32' N

Longitude: 80°36' W

Central pressure: 918 mb

Max winds: 140 knots

Airman Eaton taps us on the shoulders and points to our chairs. We all stumble back. At the eye wall again, the turbulence returns.

* * *

One o'clock in the afternoon. We make our third pass through the eye of Hurricane Ivan. The clouds part, and we can see down to a sea that is just boiling—whitecaps everywhere, huge disturbances, not a place you would want to be. If this is the eye, where things are relatively calm, it's tough to imagine what the seas must be like just outside of what we can see. A few minutes standing at the observation window, and the clouds come in again. Eaton signals to us all to sit down and get our seat belts on. A few seconds later the plane is lifted, twisted, then falls. I take a seat near the right-side scan window, and a crew man sitting next to me chuckles. "If we don't find some real turbulence for you guys, we're going to ruin our reputation."

I smile at him. "This is amazing, isn't it?" I ask.

"See what we're coming into, though?" He looks out the window, and I follow his gaze. For the first time today, I can see the wall itself. The eye is clearing, and I can see the storm turning around its open center. I raise my video camera to the window.

"Oh, I hope that shows up," I say.

"The outside of the inner eye wall," the crew man says.

"What's the pressure today?"

"Well, it's down to, it got down to 918 last time we got to go through it."

We both pause as we watch the eye wall move closer to us.

"Here comes the fun," I say.

"It's going to get kinda bumpy," he says, and I nearly laugh at his tone of voice. It's almost little-kid excited.

"Do you know what the winds are?" I ask.

"I think the highest we've seen was 141 or something like that."

"So is it a category 4 now or still a 5?"

"That's 141 knots. Still over 150 miles per hour."

"That keeps it as a category 5, then, with the winds?"

"That's probably a minimal category 5, maybe barely category 4. But they're probably not changing categories."

The clouds open for a second, and we can see the ocean again.

"What can you tell about surface winds from those wave tops?"

"You look at the waves, and you get a pretty good estimate of what the surface winds are."

"What do you think they are right now?"

"Probably 85–90 knots," he says.

Ninety knots is 104 miles an hour. Strong enough, I think. Strong enough.

The third fix is set.

Time: 0906 Zulu (2:06 PM local)

Latitude: 18°39′ N

Longitude: 80°52′ W

Central pressure: 919 mb

Max wind: 115 knots

The storm is weakening.

* * *

When turbulence comes, it comes without warning. In the back of the plane, we sit with our backs against the webbing and doze inside the drone of the engines and the comfort of a smooth flight. Then our weight nearly doubles as the plane flies through an updraft and we are pressed into our seats. When the updraft ends, pencils fly into the air as we hold on tight to our water bottles, tape recorders, cameras, and computers. Then a head-wind, and we lean hard as inertia keeps us moving forward in the slowing plane. Then smooth air. Then a hard bump as we run into or through some wind moving in some other direction. This is the roughest ride we've had all day, and it is a wonder, I think, that the plane stays together. I can tell we're getting close to the eye. I hear the dropsondes shoot out the back.

When we punch into the eye of Hurricane Ivan for the fourth time today, the eye is still ragged. Clouds race by the scan windows and porthole windows. Through open spots we can see the windblown tops of whitecapped waves. A crew member walks by and hands me a small sheet of paper. "Central Pressure 9/12" it reads at the top.

1. 888 mb Gilbert (1988)
2. 892 mb 1935 Labor Day Hurricane
3. 899 mb Allen (1980)
4–5. 905 mb Camille (1969), Mitch (1998)
6. 910 mb Ivan

The pressure reading is from early this morning, and he tells me this is the lowest-pressure storm he's ever flown through. The number above the patch on his chest tells me he has more than 3,500 hours' flying time.

The fourth fix is set.

Time: 1108 Zulu (4:08 PM local)

Latitude: 18°43' N

Longitude: 81°05' W

Central pressure: 919 mb

Max winds: 116 knots

We enter the eye wall on the far side of this pass and get the wildest ride yet. Hard up and hard down. Hard slow and then smooth air. I don't see it, but I'm told Airman Eaton is using the garbage can in the back. If I were in a commercial jet, I think, this would scare the hell out of me. I would be thinking about things like wing loading and stress fractures in the airframe, and I would be thinking about all the things we think about when we're scared—family, work, things left undone or unsaid. But somehow sitting in the belly of a wc-130 with the Hurricane Hunters, this all seems perfectly normal. This is what we expect. This is what is supposed to happen.

* * *

We're done. Scherzer tells us we're heading for home. It wasn't as rough a ride as we were expecting, he says, but the news has come in that just a little bit away from us, one of the noaa p3 Orions had a plus-3G event a few minutes ago. Now *that's* an updraft, he says.

Going through as we were at about 10,000 feet, we managed to find a smoother ride than other people today. Englehart walks through the cabin and apologizes for not finding a very well-defined eye. He said that with the media along, it's always a treat to have one. But it's still a remarkable day. Chelsea and Tom film one last segment of their report. Bellini records one last bit about the danger and risk and adventure he's been on, then goes from crew member to crew member asking them to fill in the blank. "Ivan the _____." A lot of eyes go rolling at that one.

According to the flight crew, the storm is tracking farther west than expected. "Good news for Florida," a crew member says. "Bad news for Mississippi." We both look out the scan window at nothing but gray. "But that's why we're out here," he says, "to collect all this data, get it sent back to the supercomputers. Help let people know when to prepare."

At 4:20 PM we are already back in mostly clear sky, the sea below much calmer. I'm sure if we were down there, though, we would have a different impression. We're coming up once again on the south coast of Cuba, and after that the entire Gulf Coast of the United States. We have been in the storm. Everyone below us is still waiting. But the information from this flight is already home, already in the supercomputers at the National Hurricane Center, and soon to be on the television and radio news for people in the way. A little after 6:15 PM the plane will land, and we will all say our good-byes. Chelsea and Tom will give me a ride back to the hotel on their way to edit their story, and I will watch the day's data become part of the evening's news. After the news, I will cross the street and spend a few minutes on the beach, amazed at the lack of waves. In less than two days, Hurricane Ivan, grown stronger again, will hit land nearly right on top of this hotel and Keesler Air Force Base.

For now, however, we are in the clear air over the Gulf of Mexico. I go back to the flight deck, and just stand there, looking out the large windows. No one says very much. We all find places near windows to watch the waves and sky.

3. LifeFlight

* * * *

Late summer on the prairie, evening time, and I am standing on the back porch of my house with a cup of after-dinner coffee, watching our collie run between the trees. The smell of fresh-cut grass is in the air, as is the smell of wood smoke from some neighbor's fireplace. The rising moon is just above the trees, but it's still too early for stars. This evening will be chilly. The seasons are about to change.

To the west, a line of thunderstorms fills the sky. Backlit by the setting sun, and rolling hard into and over themselves as the updrafts erupt into the fast-cooling air, the storm clouds take on colors that can worry the heart as well as the spirit: dust reds and water blues and hard-rain blacks, incredible whites and tornado greens. These storms, I think, will bring trouble. These storms, in an hour or so, could hurt. Lightning behind the storm front gives brief hints of the tremendous size of these clouds, and then a thin line of sky appears between the bottom of the storm and the horizon, and the sun illuminates the mammatus underneath. The television is already beeping warnings.

I sit on the porch step to watch the collie play and to watch the storm develop. I know I will call the dog and go inside at the last moment, perhaps just after a gust front sweeps over the yard, if only to watch this one storm and feel in my blood the rush of heavy weather. Then in the distance I hear a sound.

Softly at first, but growing louder, the unmistakable sound of a rotor cutting air. Helicopter.

It takes only a moment to find the blinking lights in the sky. Racing hard from the south, the helicopter is flying low and very fast. Urgent, I think. The maroon and white Bell 222, a twin-engine helicopter as well known to people here as the taste of snow, is the LifeFlight helicopter, an air ambulance based at Merit-Care Medical Center in downtown Fargo. MeritCare is a Level II trauma center, bigger and more capable than any other hospital within hundreds of miles, and sometimes people need to get there fast. The helicopter seems to fly every day. Somewhere in that helicopter is a person who needs help now. And with that storm approaching, that helicopter needs to get down.

The helicopter passes, the storm tests our roof and trees and floods the streets, yet after a few hours the stars are out and all is well. But I can't get the image of that race for the rooftop helipad out of my mind. In the morning, I send a quick e-mail. Dan Ehlen is the program director for LifeFlight. He knows I want to ride along. "Hi Dan," I write. "Last night I watched the helicopter come racing into town just ahead of the storm. Is there a story with last night's flight? How far out were you/they? It was a very dramatic sight . . ."

A few minutes later, the computer beeps with a reply: "There is always a story."

* * *

Of course it's dramatic. The beeper goes off, and the room gets serious. The helicopter pilot has four minutes to make a weather decision: go or no-go. If he says go, it's a race to the sky. But if he decides no-go, the medical crew still waits. If the call is for a scene flight, a flight to some roadway or farmstead or riverbank, the ground crews there will have to handle it, and the flight team goes back to what they were doing. But if the call is for a transfer from one hospital to another, in just a moment the beeper will go off again as dispatch asks the airplane pilots. If the airplane pilots say yes, an ambulance will race the medical team to the airport, and they will be gone in twenty minutes. If the airplane pilots say no too, then nobody flies. Though everyone wonders. In the United States alone, there are approximately 350,000 medical helicopter flights each year, and 100,000 flights by fixed-wing airplanes.

Six floors above the emergency room at MeritCare Hospital in Fargo, a small group of people waits in an office for the beepers on their belts to sound. In my notes, I write them down like characters in a play.

Dramatis Personae
Dan Ehlen, LifeFlight Program Director
Tim Vreeman, Pilot
Rod Wirth, Flight Paramedic
Jason Keefler, Flight Nurse and Paramedic
Nate Tiedeman, Flight Nurse
Jan Berger, Flight Nurse
Eric Castren, Flight Nurse
Charley Chamberlain, Flight Nurse

It's a mostly gray room. There's a coffeepot, a few small lockers for the crews, a round table, and some computers. There are bookshelves with binders for fixed-wing flights organized by month, rotor-wing flights, flight physiology, blood-glucose monitoring, flight-team communications, policy and procedures. There's a number of reference books on emergency care, on the Red River Valley SWAT Team standard operating procedures, and emergency nursing. There's a white dry-erase marker board for notes and comments between flights. The mugs that hang by the sink read Chronic Bronchitis, Sky Med, Med Jet. There are newsletters, thank-you cards, Christmas cards, another dry-erase board for weather conditions. There's a poster for different helicopter types

and designs. There are pictures of the crew, membership certifi-
cates from the Association of Air Medical Services, North Dakota
Ambulance licenses, pictures of the new helicopter and the old
helicopter, newspaper stories, and the Crew of the Year Award
from the American Eurocopter Corporation.

Dan's office is off to the right. Beyond that is another room
with a television and some comfortable chairs, then a small
kitchen and a hallway that leads past a bathroom and a bed-
room, past a weather computer and a large map of the United
States. A sectional map hangs by a computer just off the kitchen,
showing airports and distances, standard flight-planning stuff.
And a map of downtown Minneapolis with Post-it notes shows
the locations of the various airports and hospitals.

The hallway ends at the pilot's office. More lockers and computers. Then the door outside. There's a door next to the round
coffee table too. These doors lead to gray metal steps, then up to
the helipad and hangar and finally the machine itself. The rush
and the hope. This is just like the fire station or the ambulance
station. Only this is a hundred times more urgent, a thousand
times more complicated.

In any field there is a top of the ladder, and in emergency
response this room is it. LifeFlight averages about a thousand
flights per year, which is roughly two and a half flights every day.
For years, every time I have seen the helicopter or the airplane,
there has been a part of me that wishes, desperately, to be a part
of that rush. Speed, to save a life. Hard conditions for landing,
for taking off. Hard conditions for working the tubes and the
drugs and the monitors. Patients who do not go easily into set
procedures. Flying that goes well beyond the checklist. So one
day I simply called the office and talked with Dan. I'm working on a book, I said. I want to ride along and see what it's like.
Sounds good, he said. Come on up. He gave me a flight suit and
a fleece jacket, both with the LifeFlight name, so I would fit in
when we landed somewhere.

"But if anyone asks if you can start an IV," he said, "the answer is no."

* * *

There is a truth to the ambulance business. You wait a lot. Sometimes the calls come fast and together. Sometimes the calls don't come at all. And a truth to the northern prairie is that the weather is often too hard to fly. So there are days when I am up there, ready to fly, but all we do is sit at the round table, drink coffee, and tell stories. My small tape recorder spins in the middle.

Tim

I always liked the idea of flying. I wanted to fly. I read my first book on helicopters when I was in fifth grade. I read a biography of Igor Sikorsky. The first time I flew was in January '69. I got in a helicopter, and we took off. I graduated from flight school when I was nineteen. I turned twenty just after that. You're invincible then anyway, so it was exciting. I went through flight school—I started in an OH-23, which is a Hiller. It's a three-seat reciprocating Korean vintage helicopter. It's got a glass bubble, but it has a different tail boom from the one most people are used to seeing. Then, I got transitioned into Hueys at Fort Rucker. When I was at Fort Bragg I flew OH-13s, which was the classic M*A*S*H helicopter, and OH-23s. When I went to Vietnam, I flew Hueys. I was with the 129th Assault Helicopter Company. I flew what we called Slicks. It's a utility helicopter. You name it, we did it. We hauled people, beans and bullets, mail—all that kind of stuff. I got a total of 1,100 hours in a year—only flew 193 days in the whole year. My last 27 days, I flew 152 hours, which was a lot of hours. I never really counted, but it seemed like when I was ready to go on my R&R, which was nine months into my tour over there, it seemed like everybody was shooting at me then. Every time I'd turn around, I got shot at. Took hits three times. Technically, got shot down three times.

What do you mean by "technically"? I ask.

Well, we ended up putting the aircraft down. The aircraft was considered nonfliable because of the damage done to it. We flew it back anyway just to get it out of there. There are certain structural parts of the aircraft that, if they're damaged, you're not supposed to fly. Whatever. If it gets up and goes, it gets up and goes. I was in the service for twenty-six and a half years. In my last twenty years, I flew CH-47s, which is the largest army helicopter. In the '47s we transported personnel. We could carry thirty-three fully loaded combat troops, twenty-eight fully loaded parachutists, airborne troops, with all their gear. We could carry twenty-four litter patients with four medical attendants. We also carried tons of ammunition. We'd carry vehicles internal, guns internal. We also carried everything. We usually carried people inside, guns outside. We were also the primary mover for all nuclear weapons.

Nuclear weapons? I ask. How often did you do that?

Often enough.

What is it like to fly around here?

Weather issues here can be a problem. In the wintertime, we run into icing. I've had that happen a couple of times. Probably the most dicey situation would be thunderstorms in the summertime. We have weather radar and storm scope. But I did actually have to penetrate a line of thunderstorms once. I used the radar to see if I could get through them. After we got back, I told the flight nurse and medic that I'd never do that again. They actually put a towel over the patient's face so he wouldn't see the lightning.

But anybody on board can abort a flight. I had a flight nurse one time—we took off out of here. The weather was legal—well above minimum, actually. We took off. We got four miles on the other side of the airport. The flight nurse said, "I'm really not comfortable with this." I said, "Okay." We turned around and came back. We went by airplane.

The biggest problem with night flying around here is some of the areas that we fly into are so sparsely populated that there is no visible horizon—a really dark night or cloudy night. It's just this big black bowl.

Do you remember your first flight for MeritCare?

I can still remember my scene flight, which was down on I-94 down close to Barnesville.

What happened?

It was a single-car rollover. That happened to be a daytime flight, which was pretty good. It was kind of interesting because John Hoschied, who was the flight nurse, and then Rod Wirth was the flight paramedic, the three of us together were some of the heavyweights. We took off and went down there. It had been a long time since I had to deal with some of the winds that you have up here.

Anyway, we took off and went down there. I flew a high recon, because we were going to land on the interstate. I had to make sure that they had area cleared for us. I went back, and I did a 360. As I was coming around, I was looking out the side window, not really paying that much attention to my airspeed. I'm judging my speed by my movement across the ground. We had about a 25–30-knot wind. When I turned downwind, we're moving along pretty fast. I'm slowing up, slowing up—like I said, not looking at my airspeed indicator, I backed off the airspeed, which is no big deal until I started turning back into the wind. Then, the wind caught the vertical stabilizer, the vertical fin, and started spinning the aircraft. I started spinning pretty quick. I pushed a little of the opposite pedal to make sure I hadn't lost my tail-rotor control. It did have a little effect, so I just left it there. That thing weather-vaned. It just stopped once it turned into the wind. I pulled in some power, pushed it over. I told the crew in the back, "Sorry about that whoop-de-do back there." There wasn't anything said. They said later on that they both white-knuckled the seat.

Landing here at the hospital, if the winds are straight out of the west, that's good. Or straight out of the east—they're pretty good. If they're straight out of the north or coming out of the south, it gets pretty dicey when they're pretty strong. If it's coming out of the north, they come up the side of the building; they roll across the pad. Of course, coming out of the south, they come around the building and cause some problems. The wind limit here for us operating on and off the pad is 30 knots steady-state winds or above 30 knots or a gust spread of more than 15 knots. I've only had it once where I did not land back here with a patient. I tried twice and gave up.

Rod

My partner and I, we got a call here—it's a couple years ago now, I want to say mid-December, January—for a snowmobile accident, north of Fargo, on the Red River. We had a little bit of difficulty finding the exact spot because the information we got from dispatch said we should be north of Harwood. In all actuality, they were straight east on a big bend in the river. Two snowmobiles going opposite directions on the river came around the point and collided. Rescue was called to run the scene, and an ambulance was on the scene. They had one unresponsive driver. They wanted us to land on the river. As we were flying over the scene, just a couple hundred yards in either direction was open water on the river. I said, "No, we'll land in the field." There was no way I was going to let our pilot set that aircraft down on the ice.

Who was flying? I ask.

Sal.

Would he have landed on the river?

I don't know. Sal was born and raised in Saudi Arabia. He was . . . Rod pauses.

Ice experience a little thin? I ask.

Very. He was a guy that wore a parka in June. In the wintertime you'd see him in the back when he was working nights, and he'd have a parka on, an electric heater underneath the desk back there with gloves on trying to type on the computer. Sal and cold weather did not mix. We had to land in the field. There was deep snow on the field. Every time we'd come down there would be a whiteout. All of a sudden I'd look through the chin bubble, that window down by your feet up front, and I could see the ground moving sideways. I'd say, "Sal, we're going sideways." Three times it took us to land. Finally, when we did land, he was still moving forward. When we shut down, you could see the skid marks in the snow for quite a few yards where we didn't know we were still moving forward.

I get out—the river was on my side of the helicopter. Our partner, Marsha, gets out of the back. As she comes around the front of the aircraft, all of a sudden she goes up to about her waist in the snow because right there was a farm drainage ditch. No way to see it—the snow was that deep. Right in front of the aircraft. The snow was deep. We got over to the river. It's a steep bank going down to the river, trees, but the rescue crew had waved me to come on over here. I had some of our equipment. I started down. All of a sudden, I looked back. All I could see of Marsha is the top of her just below her chin on up. She had stepped in and she was right to the deep.

Do you guys wear cold-weather gear when you go out on winter rescues? I ask.

Coats, over the top—nothing other than what we got on other than coats. When it's real cold, I've got thermal underwear and stuff like that. We finally got down to the ice to where the patient was. Ambulance crews were down there. The guy needed to be intubated. They were having difficulty. We didn't know if he had a c-spine fracture, and we have to maintain stabilization in trying to intubate him. It was hard. When you get a coating of blood on the tip of the laryngoscope bulb, it gets dark. I was having trouble. Finally, they had a Combitube laying there. It's a blind insertion. You put it in, and then you have two balloons that you inflate. If it doesn't go in the trachea, it will go in the esophagus—one or the other. Depending on which area it's in, it makes a difference on which of the two tubes that are sticking out of the mouth that you ventilate through.

The Combitube normally has a kind of a curl to it. It was cold, probably somewhere between 0 and 10 below that day. I'm laying on my stomach trying to intubate this guy. Just couldn't get a good visualization of the cords I could use because of the blood and everything else. They had the Combitube laying there that they had tried to put in. I figured—well, I'd go ahead and use that. I'm trying to get it in. I noticed that it didn't seem like it had enough of its natural curve, so I reached over and had to put a little bit of a curve in it. It's plastic. It broke!

Go back to the laryngoscope; try it again. I did get the guy intubated. Then it was such a job getting him from the river, back up the steep riverbank, through the trees. He's on a backboard. You've got all this dead and fallen wood underneath the snow. We go up in levels. We'd sit there. We bagged this guy a few times. One of the rescue-squad people would reach down and grab my arm, pull me up to the next level. They would reach down, pull me up about four feet up the bank, and then we'd have other people who would hand the board up to the next group of guys. I bagged this patient some more. The crews would kind of rotate. They'd pull me up four feet, reach down, bring the patient up four feet. That's the way we went. It was probably fifty feet up this bank. The snow was anywhere from three to six feet deep in places. What I said out there on the ice that day was not recorded.

What happened to Marsha? I ask.

When she was coming down the bank, a couple of those snowmobilers kind of helped her out.

Tim

Some of the interesting ones—we had a scene flight down southwest of here one time. It was a single-motorcycle accident. The guy had been out riding his motorcycle and hit a pothole and lost control of the bike, went off the road, and somersaulted over the handlebar. He was a heavy guy. He's three hundred pounds, truck driver. When he somersaulted, he didn't have a helmet on, but that wasn't his problem. When he did the somersault, he actually landed on both feet and shattered both lower legs. He was laying out there by himself for a while till somebody drove by and saw the motorcycle there. They called 911. They called for us. We got out there. On a scene flight when we land, we don't shut the aircraft down. The pilot sits in there with the aircraft running. I was sitting there waiting and waiting and waiting. I looked over to the ambulance. There was nothing going on in the ambulance. I couldn't understand it. I couldn't see any movement. They had already gotten him out of the ditch. And there was a pickup truck parked in front of the ambulance. All of a sudden I saw the flight nurse stand up with an IV bag and stuff like that. They had him in the back of the pickup truck. That's how they brought him over to the aircraft.

* * *

The beepers go off at 1:00 p.m. Medical patient, a transfer from Bemidji, Minnesota.

Tim walks to the weather computer and calls up the information. At Fargo, the wind is from the northwest, 350 degrees, at 14 knots. Visibility is 10 statute miles. At Bemidji, the wind is from the northwest, 360 degrees, at 9 knots. Visibility there is 10 statute miles as well. Clear skies in both places. Bright sunshine. It's a beautiful early-spring day on the prairie. Snow still covers the fields and farmsteads, but the rivers are opening and the snow is melting fast.

At 1:02 PM, Tim dials dispatch and says the flight is a go. He changes his ball cap for a knit cap to wear under his helmet and puts on a vest, and then we are out the door and up the stairs. Rod and Jason are already there, ready to load a cot into the helicopter.

They stay with the cot and medical supplies while Tim and I go into the hangar. The helicopter rests on a battery-powered dolly, and once the hangar door is open, one man can throw a switch and walk the helicopter to the pad more easily than he can turn a push mower around a tree. Once in place, the dolly is lowered and taken away. Rod and Jason load their supplies while Tim does a final walk-around. Jason asks if I want to sit up front.

A security guard from the hospital, dressed all in black, appears with a battery pack to help start the engines. His eyes scan the pad and helicopter, looking for debris and making sure everything is closed and tight. Then the deep whine starts as the engines come alive, a rising pitch. At 24 percent power, the blades begin to turn. Tim signals the security guard, who disconnects the battery pack and disappears inside the building.

In my headset, I can hear ATIS, the automated tower information system, give the current weather information. And I watch Tim flex his hands around the controls.

In a helicopter, the lever that makes the thing go up and down is called the collective. It sits to the left of the pilot, like a parking brake on the wrong side, and he uses his left hand and arm to move it. The control between his legs, where a normal stick or yoke would be in an airplane, is called the cyclic, and it makes the helicopter go forward or back, or left or right. And whereas helicopters have aft rotors instead of rudders, they are both controlled by foot pedals, and the result is the same.

Tim pulls back on the collective slightly, and I can feel the rotors bite more deeply into the air. We are airborne, two or three feet off the helipad deck. He turns us into the wind, hovers, and radios the tower at Hector Field to let them know we are departing, heading northeast to Bemidji.

You are clear to depart at your own risk, the controller says.

Your own risk? I ask.

We're not at the airport, Tim says. So technically they can't clear us for anything.

Tim pushes the cyclic forward just a bit to lower the nose and give us some forward speed, and he pulls back on the collective to keep us in the air. We move forward, and, suddenly clear of the rotor wash and ground effect at the pad, the air is smooth and we accelerate over the hospital and then the trees and homes of north Fargo. In the back, Rod calls dispatch at FM Ambulance and tells them our departure time and our destination. He ends with a count: "Four souls on board."

This trip, however, is a setup. A deception. A ruse. Fifteen minutes ago, Dan walked out of his office and told everyone we were going to run a downed-aircraft drill. In essence, we were going to take off, fly a short distance, and then disappear. The purpose of the drill was to see how the dispatchers at FM Ambulance handled our disappearance. There's a long list of protocols, and they need to follow them all.

We turn northeast and climb to 2,500 feet. Once clear of town, below us snowmobile tracks in the snow surround farmhouses. We pass wind-driven power generators and radio towers. Tim points out the towns of Averill and Ulen and Hitterdahl, then hands me a sectional chart, the map for pilots, so I can follow the waypoints and mark them for my own flying.

I ask him about standard procedures for takeoff and landing.

In a helicopter, he says, it's airspeed over altitude. You want airspeed more than you want altitude. When we take off, we accelerate to 40 knots, then pitch to climb at 60 to 70 knots. We have to be 300 feet above ground level before we make any turn. Landing, we shoot for an 8 percent angle of approach. A shallow approach is 3 to 5 percent. A steep approach, if we're landing in someone's yard, for example, and have to get over the trees, can be pretty much anything. Sometimes we hover and let the rotor wash clear away a bunch of snow before we land.

In my headset, I can hear air traffic control (ATC) as well as Rod and Jason. Radio and intercom. But then I hear an ambulance talking to the hospital too. Tim tells me they monitor the Minnesota State Emergency Frequency as well as the North Dakota State Emergency Frequency and the state emergency medical services (EMS). I can cut any of them out, he says, but it's nice to know what's going on.

I look over my shoulder at Rod and Jason. Both are looking out the windows at the bright snowfields and the cloudless sky.

What would you be doing if this were a real flight? I ask.

Enjoying the view, says Rod.

Jason explains that if they knew what type of patient they were receiving, they might prep certain IVs or other stuff. It could save two or three minutes, he says.

But then Rod smiles and repeats himself. Enjoy the view.

Tim begins to explain the instruments, the Garmin 430 GPS system, the Bendix weather radar, the storm scope to spot lightning, but I find myself agreeing with Rod. It is a beautiful day.

Rod calls back to dispatch with a position report. And once they answer, Tim smiles. Time to disappear, he says. He turns the helicopter around to fly back to Fargo, but he also pulls a switch that removes us from the computer screen in the dispatch control room. Now they don't know where we are, he says, and we're not going to tell them.

Landing at the hospital, we face into the wind until we hover a few feet over the pad. Then Tim turns us nose to the hospital and sets us down. Nose left, tail right, he says into the intercom.

The medical crew is supposed to help watch for obstacles when landing and taking off. Then in my headset I hear dispatch call, wondering where we are. Jason says, We'll see how far down the procedures they get.

Rod and Jason go inside. Tim refuels the helicopter, then rolls the dolly out of the hangar and positions it under the helicopter. A flick of a switch and the helicopter is lifted, and Tim rolls it back into the hangar.

Downstairs, Dan is not very happy with the drill. The dispatcher did not follow procedure, although what she did made sense. Instead of following the protocol, she simply called Bemidji to ask if we were there. Whomever she got on the phone was not the person who knew a drill was under way. We're not expecting them, the person in Bemidji said. Oh, okay, said dispatch.

Rod hurries through the room and looks at me. Are you coming with us? he asks.

Where?

Fixed-wing flight, Grand Forks to Rochester, he says.

I look at my watch, and think of the obligations at home.

I can't, I say. And then he's gone.

Jason

We were doing a scene flight one day for a motor vehicle crash, and the patient was ejected from the vehicle. The patient was unresponsive. We didn't know they were unresponsive until we got there and assessed him. The patient was unresponsive, laying there in the middle of this field. I think it was in the summer. There was no snow or anything on the ground. We were probably a good hundred yards off the highway. I had my intubation stuff, started to intubate this patient, and had to maintain head stabilization so we don't hurt the neck at all. Attempted the first intubation. I didn't get it. I pulled back, started to bag him. I set down my tube in the bag. I turned around to reintubate, and my tube is gone! Where did it go? I just grabbed another one, opened it up, got it all set up, and went to intubate again. When I came to intubate that time, the guy was starting to wake up a little bit. When I went to pull the tube out, he had actually bit the balloon off the end of the tube. I set that one down, and then it was gone! Well, I couldn't use it anyway. But I thought, "Where do my tubes keep going?" Finally, I grabbed another tube. My partner had run back to grab the monitor. When he came back, we went to tube the guy. Turns out one of the people that was around and trying to help thought that everything that I set down was trash. So he kept throwing it in the field! Everything I set down. He was trying to help me. He's throwing this stuff I need. Every time I set something down, it was gone. He saw me use it once. He didn't know what it was for. He saw me use it, thought it was no good anymore, and tossed it. I ended up going through three or four tubes, and every time I set one down he thought it was trash!

My partner was coming back from the helicopter and saw where the guy was grabbing stuff. I was focused on the patient, and I have stuff all around me. I was looking all over! Good God, we laughed!

I had another flight. It was a scene flight. It was a bystander—no, it was a first-responder, one of those really helpful first-responders. I hand him an IV bag, and he becomes a human IV pole. Those are the people you don't want to move. But they're the ones that, whenever you ask for anything, they are the ones that will grab it first. So I'd ask for something, and this guy with the IV would run—and out your IV goes! It didn't happen once; it happened twice. Same guy, same thing. It's like, why do I need to keep putting IVs in this patient? It didn't make any difference to the outcome of the patient. Still, I was thinking . . .

From across the office, Rod calls, No amount of tape is enough.

We've heard about every bad word you can possibly imagine, Jason says. We get calls to put in ivs all over the hospital. Wearing a flight suit, we get the most weird responses when we walk in. What part of the military are you in? The best one was when I walked in and said, "My name is Jason. I'm going to . . ." And the guy said, "What's a mechanic doing in here?"

Janitor, says Rod.

I didn't know pilots started ivs!

Both men laugh.

Then again, I got called to do an iv another time on this general medical floor. We get called to do difficult ivs all the time. Two women in two beds. I got called in there, and I started the first gal's iv. I talked to her. She said, "Thanks." I left. About ten minutes later I got called back up to the same room. Man, I think, I know that iv was good. I get up there. She had told her roommate that I did such a good job that I should come and start her iv too. As I'm walking out the room, the first one says, "So, how does it feel to do two women in the same room?" They were younger gals. They were just rolling. I'm just bright red walking away!

Dan

Probably the most memorable flight I was ever on, the reason I remember it, we flew in to pick up a, I believe he was probably about twelve years old, severely burned patient, from a very small emergency room. The physician there was mishandling the case, so of course we had to come in and take care of the child.

Did the physician know he was mishandling? Did he call you? I ask.

Yes, he did call. A severely injured child needed to be transported to a larger facility, and we do that because people in these small facilities just can't handle something like that. The facilities themselves aren't set up to handle someone that severely injured. So naturally we're called to come in. What happened was that the physician was mishandling the case. Everybody in the entire hospital knew it. Very small town. The whole town was there, ambulance service was all there, all of the relatives were all there, and they all knew. And even before we got in the doors, people said, "Now you guys are here, you have to do something. He doesn't know what he's doing."

Literally, I ask, can you take over that way?

Let me tell you the rest of the story. We walked in, and here this doctor has a couple of people trying to hold this child down, putting a breathing tube down his throat. If you put an endotracheal tube through somebody's vocal chords, obviously they can't talk. They put this tube down this child's throat, who then sat up and said, "Why are you doing this to me?" Obviously, he put it in the wrong spot. Once we saw that, we were taking over the care of this child. Normally we don't do that. No matter how badly somebody is being mismanaged, we try to go in and make that physician think that's the best care we've ever seen anybody have, even though they've totally screwed up. You know, just for PR purposes. This is one case we just couldn't do that. We said no, you need to get out of our way. It doesn't matter what you say. I have a duty to intervene when you mismanage.

Rod

Eric and I were up north to Baudette one time. We picked up a patient that wasn't doing real well respiratory-wise. We talked to him and explained what we were going to have to do. We were going to have to intubate him. We'd give him some medication to put him to sleep, which now I tell him the medication is going to make him real sleepy. We got him intubated. We flew him down here. He was on a ventilator down ICU for about six weeks before they woke him back up. They kept him sedated for that long because of his condition. I just happened to stop down there. This gentleman's name was Stanley. Just happened to stop down there in the ICU and walked in to say hi. I said, "Do you remember me?" He goes, "Yes, I remember you. You're the son of a bitch who said, 'Good night, Stanley,' and that's the last thing I remembered for six weeks!" Then he starts laughing and thanking us for taking such good care of him. It's times like that make things worthwhile, too.

But there are lots of stories which aren't funny at all. We had a little eight-month-old patient we flew in the fixed wing from here down to the Cities. She went into cardiac arrest while we were on final approach to St. Paul. Eight months old. We're doing CPR and kneeling on the floor of the airplane, kneeling against the bench, intubating her as the wheels hit the runway. The guys from Life Link III, the ambulance service down in St. Paul that always picks us up, they opened up the door. "Hey, how're you guys doing?" they called. I hollered, "Get in here. We need some help." I'm holding the tube, bagging this little one, and the nurse is doing compressions. We had the parents in the plane with us.

Screaming? I ask.

No, they were very calm, very composed. This little one had some serious medical problems. She needed a kidney. This was in the spring. They were waiting until later in the fall when they were going to try and give her one of her father's kidneys. She was sick. High temp. They wanted to get her down to the hospital at the U of M. We stood out there on the ramp. We got her out of the airplane. The Life Link III had their cot sitting there. There were two nurses. They're helping us. They got interosseous IVs put in. We're giving her meds and coding this little one. Another one of their crews had heard what was going on because they had radioed for the helicopter to come from the other side of the airport to pick us up to take us to the hospital instead of going back. One of the other crews that was from St.

Paul's Children's, which is just a matter of a few blocks from the airport, who was in the ER, heard them talking about what was going on. They had a peds intensivist in the ER. They said, "Hey, you want to go for a ride with us?" Explained what the deal was. They jumped in the ambulance. They come screaming over to the airport. By the time they got that doctor there, we already had a pulse back on this little one and a heartbeat. We're out there working, and Molly was the copilot and Harland was the pilot. We had one standing on one end of the cot being a human IV pole. The other one was standing on the other end of the cot holding our drug kit, being a human shelf. They were both whiter than that paper. We got the little one back. En route to the hospital, we lost pulse again. They coded the little one there, and St. Paul Children's got her back. She did die the next day.

That was the one time when I came back here and seriously thought about maybe a career of flipping burgers at McDonald's was where I should be.

Tim

We normally cruise about 130 knots, roughly 150 miles per hour. Red line is 150 knots, which is 170 miles an hour. We get whatever. The way we fly is we fly a power setting. That way, everything is constant. Wear and tear on the aircraft is constant; the fuel flow is constant. That way we maintain a constant cost. We use 85 percent power. We set it and get whatever airspeed we can get based on that power set. Our airspeed does vary a little bit. Air conditions and stuff. I've had ground speed—I had it one time where coming back from Britton with a patient on board at night and racing a thunderstorm. We had a tailwind coming back. I was doing 167 knots indicated ground speed. I started my deceleration at West Acres Mall, so we could slow it down and turn right. One of the guys who used to be here, he came back from Jamestown one night. He had 193-knot ground speed. But sometimes we have a headwind too. I had to fly back in the aircraft coming back from Sisseton one time. John Hoschied happened to be the flight nurse that night. We took off. We were coming back, and I was watching ground speed on the GPS, and it kept getting slower and slower. John said, "Is that Wahpeton out there?" I said, "Yeah." About fifteen minutes later, he said, "Is that Wahpeton out there?" I said, "Yeah."

Dan

I had a flight one time, and this guy is really, really sick. He needs to fly back. He's having a heart attack. He says, "I don't want to fly." I said, "You really need to fly. If you don't fly, you're probably going to die." He says, "I don't want to fly. I don't want to fly." We kind of made him come out to the airport. As we're putting him into the little helicopter, he puts his hands up. He says, "God damn it. I'm not flying with you guys." We sedated him a little bit and got him in the aircraft because, if we didn't fly him, he's going to die. The damn old guy showed us. He died. He didn't want to fly so bad that he just died rather than get in that damn helicopter. We ended up not going anyplace. As soon as we got him in the helicopter and closed the door, he died because he did not want to fly. He really didn't.

Jan

I started out flying in Aberdeen, South Dakota. Before that, I was a homemaker and decided to go to nursing school to be an OB nurse. That's what I wanted to do. If I was ever going to go to nursing school and be a nurse, I was going to be an OB nurse. I did. I worked OB for seven years. It just so happened that my director had moved. We had an interim director on our OB unit, who was also the ER director. We were just kind of sitting around talking one afternoon. I always liked the high-risk

OB patients, the Level II babies—the little more critical, a little more excitement, a little more heart rush, a little bit more intense. She said, "You know, you should try ER. You would really like that." I said, "No way. I didn't get into this to do emergency medicine." "No, really you ought to try it. You really should." She kind of egged me on for a couple weeks. Suddenly, I thought, What's it going to hurt? I ought to try it. I went part-time in the ER and dropped back to part-time in OB. I kept my foot in the door there in case I hated it. I've been in emergency medicine ever since—didn't leave.

And so you moved into flying from there. What was the attraction? I ask.

The higher level of thinking, the critical-care skills that you need, the autonomy, being the primary caregiver in a situation where maybe they haven't care yet at a scene flight or whatever—that kind of thing. A huge, huge draw to people in crisis. You're in a car accident—obviously, you didn't plan to have it happen. All of a sudden, you're having your absolutely worst day. There's something about going in there and saying, "Hey, I'm here. I'm going to help you." Giving them some kind of comfort, then having the knowledge to be able to do that. It's all just kind of "Whew."

Do you remember your first flight? I ask.

Oh, yeah, like it was yesterday. It was interesting. It was a pretty routine flight. It was a gentleman actually, who had a fall—an elderly gentleman—and he needed a head CT. We flew him down to Sioux Falls. For me, it was kind of like, okay, this is your time that you can get used to what you're doing. I said it was pretty straightforward. It was at night. It was at 1:30 in the morning. It was February 18. You don't forget that kind of stuff. It was a full moon. It was absolutely gorgeous out. Snow on the ground. Actually, we could see our helicopter shadow in the snow because the moon was so bright. Oh, gosh, it was gorgeous.

But there was another one, my second flight position, after hospital orientation, which is just paperwork, in Denver. The very first night on the job we got there at 6:30. It started with, "Hi, how are you? This is our office. Here's the coffeepot." That kind of stuff. At 7:02 we got paged out to a scene flight on the interstate. It was a car accident, a six year old unconscious. We had tons of equipment. I hadn't even touched any of it, let alone even seen it. I think it was about four or five minutes to get to the scene. The gentleman who was orienting said, "Okay, you're going to intubate." Okay. I'm just rummaging through. That was, you know, a six year old. It was a big deal. I just remember that because it's 7:02, never been in the aircraft, never seen any of their equipment, and boom! Got out there, got him intubated.

And there are always the nightmare flights. The ones where you're going EEK! You're doing fifty thousand things at once. You get there and it's like, oh, we're already at least ten steps behind the eight ball.

Have you lost patients? I ask.

You know I hadn't until, boy, it wasn't very long. I was working in Colorado about a week. They had a bad car accident north of Denver, a small town, five to six hundred people. Five kids riding in a pickup at noon hour. They were all in the cab—all shoved in the cab. It was one of those places in Colorado, just east of Rocky Mountain National Forest. It was flat. It was like a little flat prairie land between the mountains. They got going a good clip, rolled the vehicle. Two were dead at the scene. We got called for two. I was working up in the mountains that day in Frisco. They dispatched us, and they dispatched Air Life Denver, who is another helicopter service in Denver. We took turns. We got there first. We took the most critical one, who was a seventeen year old with a closed head injury. Not good. It was a twenty-three- or twenty-four-minute flight to Poudre Valley, which is the closest to a trauma center that we were going to. We were in flight must have been not even ten minutes—six or seven minutes—she coded. At seventeen years old, it's like, man, come on. I said to my pilot, "How far out are we?" "Seventeen minutes." Your heart just sinks. We ran the code until we got there. She didn't make it. That one always sticks in my mind. You go back and say, "I couldn't have done anything different." It was just the way it's going to be.

I had another one of those right before I left Colorado. It was a seven year old who was riding on the back of an ATV. Her uncle got off. She was going to scoot up toward the handlebars. She grabbed the handlebars and whoom! It reared up on her like a horse. It was a 750-pound ATV four-wheeler and landed on top of her. She had a bad closed head injury. We got to the scene and intubated her. Took her to Children's. It was only a twelve-minute flight. That was a bad outcome, too. She didn't make it. She had twelve cranial fractures and herniated her brain stem. There's nothing you can do. You just feel so helpless. It's like—if I could just do something else. You can't. That one still breaks my heart.

But there are the funny moments, too. This didn't happen to me, but it was a coworker of mine. I'm glad it wasn't me. It was funny, but I think it was funny because it wasn't me. She went out to pick up a patient, a rendezvous with a ground ambulance. It was a seventeen year old with stroke symptoms. Bilateral weakness in arms and legs, numbness, tingling, weakness. She got there and ended up transporting him back. But she felt like a fool. Turns out, he had just broken up with his girlfriend and had hyperventilated.

When you look at putting on that flight suit, you would think you'd have this feeling, this huge sense of accomplishment. It's heavier than it looks. Along with the flight suit comes all that responsibility. You are it. You're responsible. You have to take control. The first time I put it on, the second I put it on, it was like ah . . . this isn't quite the feeling. I like it, but this isn't quite the feeling, I thought. It really was a humbling experience. I thought it was going to be like a career high. It knocked me down several notches, like, whoa, now I've really got to be on my game. I've got all this responsibility. People are looking at me and saying, "Okay. What do we do here?" It is a huge responsibility. That never goes away, for me anyway. You hear a lot of people get that sense of indestructibility, that teenage kind of stuff. Thank God I've never been struck by that. It's always been, I thank God that I'm able to wear it. I take it extremely seriously. Every little thing that I can learn to help me along the way. It's pretty amazing. I couldn't do anything else. Somebody asked me one time, "How long are you going to be a flight nurse?" Until I can't anymore. I can't imagine going back to doing anything else.

Rod

I usually carry our pins for the little kids. We're all out of them right now. I used the last one yesterday. It started out early last summer. We flew up to rural North Dakota, Rolla, to take this little girl down to Minneapolis to the Children's Hospital. She had some type of infection in the pelvic bone. We got there in her room. I was talking to her. She's about six years old and scared. I was kneeling down in front of her, and I asked her if she wanted to go flying with us. She shook her head yes. She was quite a little piece of cake there. I asked her, "Well, do you have wings?" She shook her head. I said, "Little girls can't unless they have wings. I think I've got an extra pair." I pulled this pin out and hooked it on her little hospital gown. It breaks you down right there. They have fun. Yesterday we flew a little seven year old in from Bemidji. I had to do the same thing with her. She was just a little sweetheart after that.

Tim

We get quite a few people come up. A lot of times the kids—the families will bring the kids up because they want to see the helicopter. We'll bring them up and give them a tour. There was a gentleman who came up here. We had transported his wife. They came up to see the helicopter. They had their daughter and son with. The son was like five or six. The little girl was four years old. She was gorgeous, just a gorgeous little girl. They were getting ready to leave, and I said, "My wife would love to have you come home with me and stay with us. Would like to come home with me?" She said, "No, but you can take my brother."

* * *

The inventory is impressive. Dan hands me sheet after sheet of paper that details what the helicopter carries. Something called a LifePak. Two oxygen flowmeters. Two oxygen hookups. Two vacuum outlets with disposable suction canisters. Bath blanket, pillow, sheet, towel. Wolfsburgh Radio. Two patient stretchers. Ventilator. Bedpan, urinal, garbage bags, emesis basin, toilet paper, suction canisters, latex gloves. Goggles. Coveralls. Tube Salem Sump. Tube feeding. KY Jelly. Lidocaine jelly. Pressure infuser. Bandages and sponge gauze and something called a Primary Micro Safety/Clave. There is an Intertech "Peep" valve, and a "Peep" valve adapter. There are adult oral airways in large and medium and small. An Airway Combi Esophageal. Limb restraints adult disp. Heimlich valves. Disposable scalpel with no. 10 blade. Needles and suture. A skin stapler. A Tracheal Hook Jackson One Prong. An iv-start kit. Syringes of every size. Alcohol wipes. Betadine wipes. Band-Aids. A VixOne nebulizer. Blood tubing. Four different sizes of laryngoscope, as well as a laryngoscope lightbulb replacement and a laryngoscope handle, large. Forceps. Size C batteries. Tongue depressors.

These are just the things that make sense to me. The inventory lists row after row of equipment I cannot begin to imagine. The tube endo 8.0 ring pull, for example. I could go to medical school, I think, to figure this out.

And then there are the drugs. Listed alphabetically, the adult drug pack begins with Adenosine and ends with Verapamil, with Albuterol, Atropine, Benzatropine, Diphenhydramine, Fentanyl, Heparin, Hydromorphone, Lidocaine, Morphine, Nitroglycerin, Propranolol, and at least a dozen more in between. The pediatric drug pack begins with Acetaminophen, Albuterol, Ampicillin, and Atropine and ranges through Diazepam and Diphenhydramine and Dopamine to Fentanyl and Gentamicin to Insulin and Lidocaine to Morphine and Phenobarbital and ends with Sterile Water and Succinylcholine, again with many in between. There are channel blockers and ACE inhibitors and nitrates.

There is the survival equipment, in case the helicopter goes down. Compass. Aerial flares. Panel markers. Highway safety flares. Signal mirror. Strobe light. Tent. Sleeping bags. Saw and shovel and hunting knife. String. Matches and fire sticks. Three ready-to-eat meals. An empty coffee can. Aircrew survival manual.

If the helicopter goes down, one crew member tells me, we don't need to worry about food.

Why is that? I ask.

If the helicopter goes down, we have no further use for a pilot, he says.

I learn the helicopter carries much more than a standard ground ambulance, because the helicopter is classified as a critical-care unit. Critical care in a machine with a top speed of 170 miles an hour. The patients could begin in any condition. A medical transfer whose needs are beyond wherever they are, or someone who's just been cut out of an overturned car. Sometimes the flight crew takes them to the ER, or direct to one of the ICUS. There are even occasions when the patient goes straight down to the cardiac catheterization lab. But in between, in the time of all possible speed, anything can happen. What they carry is the list for anything.

Tim

From the time we're paged to make a weather decision, whether it's a go or no-go, we limit ourselves to four minutes. We allow five; we limit ourselves to four. From the go to takeoff is actually ten minutes. We usually make it in from six to eight minutes. It only takes a minute, or less, to push the helicopter back out of the hangar. Maybe a minute or less. It depends on how much we have to jockey the aircraft. If the wind is real strong out of the west or north, we'll have to jockey the aircraft a little more. It takes a little longer. If it's just going straight out—about thirty seconds, it's on the deck and ready to go.

Eric

I remember one specifically where we were responding out in rural Minnesota. It was at night on the weekend. It was a two-motorcycle, one-vehicle accident. There were multiple injuries. We got there before the ambulance ground crews did. We just happened to be in that distance.

So who was there? Highway patrolmen? I ask.

They could have been there. I probably would have walked right by them. I didn't recognize them. There were bikes lying all over the ground. There were people lying here and crews running to them. It actually looked almost surreal. It almost looked like a goofy scene from a movie—a bad movie—that you've seen. It was quite a deal. We were right there. We had a very short ground time.

Everyone happened to get on the ground at the same moment. People were still trying to account for people. They weren't quite sure where everyone was and if they found everyone. It doesn't happen very often. That was about as quick as we've been on a scene that I've been involved in. It just happened to work that way. Some bystander called at the farmhouse and watched everybody at the same time. We just happen to get there first. Somebody says, "We've got this one—go to that one; go to the next one." We went to the next one. You're focusing on what you're doing. I can hear in the background, it's like we can't find so-and-so. There are flashlights out in the field. People are looking. You're doing your stuff here, and they're still trying to find a person who they think may or may not be missing. They don't know. It was one of my first interesting scene flights. Since then, we've had quite a few. They're all interesting as far as that goes. Scene flights charge you up a little bit more.

But you can have just as bad or complicated interfacility transports as far as medical patients. In fact, trauma seems to be a little bit easier. When you know you've got a mechanism of injury, you're either going to see the injuries or find the injuries or you're not going to find them. Hopefully, you do find them. In some of those things, you've got bleeding. You replace the blood, you stop the bleeding. It's pretty easy to do. When you start dealing with long-term medical issues and stuff on the transfer flights, sometimes these are people who have been sick for quite some time with multiple medical diagnoses. All of a sudden, they drop in blood pressure or drop in this or that. It may not be caused by one item. It could be caused by a multitude of medical conditions and trying to figure out and detect what that may be is actually more challenging.

Charley

It takes a lot of energy to do this job. It takes a lot of energy to do the floor-nursing jobs or working in ER. I do work some shifts in the emergency room because I like that, too. Because you have a variety. That's different from a floor, because part of the thing about this job is the unknown. They may tell you that the patient you're going for is fourteen years old. You get there, and he's four years old. You have to be flexible, very flexible, to adjust your train of thought to the patient that you're transporting at the time. I've had four helicopter flights in one day, and one will be a scene flight, another one will be an eighty year old and have a cardiac problem, and another one will be an OB flight, a mom with maybe premature rupture of membranes who needs to come here for the ICU, the next one will be an aneurysm, somebody with a head leak or unconscious and intubate him. You have to adjust.

Eric

I remember one time we went on a King Air flight to Bemidji. It was funny. We went to pick up a trauma patient. That particular patient was long-boarded and c-collared and strapped on the cot. We were on our way back; it's myself and another man and two pilots. These pilots were great. It was just funny. It struck me as hilarious. The pilot gets on the intercom. He says, "You know what? There's a little bit of weather." It's only about a twenty-minute flight. "I'm going to deviate a little further south to get away from this cell." It wasn't maybe three minutes after that. It felt like the hand of God had hit us. It felt like we had just gotten beaten straight into the ground. It was just one jolt. It was enough. I had glanced over. The backboard on the cot was strapped tight to our cot. But I saw it raise like an inch. You swear these things are tight. I could have sworn I just heard a pop up in the air. I had hit my head on the ceiling. I didn't have my seat belt on. I looked around and saw the medic I was with. His headset had moved all the way around about 90 degrees. Chin strap right about there. Naturally, we have a way to communicate with the pilots. I pushed the button. I go, "Was that expected? I'm glad you deviated so we could avoid that." I was giving him a hard time. I go, "What's the first thing that came out of your mouth?" He goes, "Mommy." It was funny. We never felt anything before. We didn't feel anything after.

Nate

I like the ems stuff. I like where you don't know what's coming
in, think on your feet, a lot of patient changeover. Coming in,
like when I worked in the icu, you'll have the same patient for
two or three weeks, where in the er, you have a rapid change-
over. Your day is always a little bit different. In the icu or even
some of the general floors, you can kind of plan your day out.
It's kind of the same thing. I'm not a big planner by any means.
I'm a fly-by-the-seat-of-your-pants. I don't like schedules. I just
like to go with the flow.

Do you remember your first scene flight? I ask.

Haven't had one yet.

You're kidding.

That is one of the things in my orientation I didn't get. I was
close. Last week, we did a ground intercept where we hooked
up with fm Ambulance and intercepted with Mahnomen Ambulance north of Detroit Lakes. It was a patient who was in a
Chevy four door truck pulling a fifth wheel, went into the ditch,
rolled four times. She was restrained, had massive intrusion on
the topside of the vehicle, and she was brought to Mahnomen
Health Center. We weren't able to get there by helicopter. We
don't fly there by fixed wing because it takes too long for us
to get to the airport, fly up there, and land. The time doesn't
make sense to fly fixed wing there. We did a ground intercept
just north of Detroit Lakes. We meet them where we meet them.
Once we see their lights, we just spin around on the road. We
take all of our equipment with us, jump out of the ambulance
we're in, get into the ambulance the patient is in at that time.
That was my first pretty unstable trauma patient. This patient
was unresponsive and had a massive head injury, had a cricothyrotomy because they weren't able to intubate the patient orally.
Normally, when we put a breathing tube in, we put it through
their mouth, into their trachea, into their windpipe. This patient,

because of the trauma to her face and the ratio, it's called, on her intubation stats, they had to do a cricothyrotomy, where it's like a surgical airway—they cut down through the throat, into their cricoid membrane, and pass an intubation or an ET tube right into the trachea from there. This patient also developed a pneumothorax, which is the air trapping between the chest wall and the lung. It creates tension. They are unable to breathe very well. That was my first chest tube that I ever put in on a patient. It went very well for the first time. I was pretty pumped and excited that my partners let me do that. We brought her here to the trauma center at Fargo. It's not really a scene flight, but it's my first pretty unstable trauma patient, which was an excellent experience for me on my orientation.

Have you done a lot of medical-transfer flights? I ask. Any flights at all?

The reason I'm called the "anchor" is because I never fly anywhere. Nothing's going to happen when I'm on. It's the same way when I worked on the ambulance. It's just never busy. I don't know if you want to call it the best luck or the worst luck. It depends on how you want to look at it. I want to fly. I want to get the experience. I want to get the critical patients. I would say, roughly, I've been on probably a dozen flights. Give or take a few here or there during my orientation. I've had two flights since I've been off my orientation, which was this week.

So what do you think so far?

My wife is so sick of me in the last two months. This is all I talk about. That's it. My dad—we were playing cards with my dad last night. He finally said, "That's enough." I don't even think of it. Someone says "chair" and I'm like, "Yeah, we flew to Lisbon this day, and there was a chair in the corner, but this patient . . ." Anything I can tie together with my flight experience I've had in the last two months, I've been doing.

And I remember the first thing my mom said to me: "How can you handle it? You're kind of high-strung." I don't like to sit. I like to move. That's why I like our ER here. There's nights on a twelve-hour shift you don't sit down. Moving, thinking, talking. I was just down on 2 East. One of my friends, who's a clinical instructor who used to work in the ER, he goes, "Are you bored yet?" I said, "Well, yeah, but the anticipation inside keeps me going a little bit." He goes, "God, that'd be great. To do nothing for twelve hours and get paid for it." I said, "Yeah, but this is the way I look it. You know cops are overpaid 80 percent of the time and couldn't pay them enough for that last 20." It's the same way I think on flight. In that 20 percent of the time, you couldn't pay me enough. Just the two of us to deal with what a team of thirty does here for a call. That's pretty intense. I know I know my stuff, but then there's always that question in my mind, "Do I really know it as well as I think I do?" This is something that I've had—not a hard time or difficult time. I like positive things. You're doing a good job—great job. Like I said to Rodney yesterday, "How am I doing?" He goes, "Well, when you're doing bad, I'll let you know." So, I'm doing okay? Yeah. Okay. All right. I need to prove it to myself.

* * *

The beepers go off at 9:57 AM. This one is no drill. Adult trauma, the beeper screen reads. Valley City to Fargo. Patient weight 180 pounds.

It's a clear, bright day in Fargo, and has been all morning, and all yesterday. The forecast is for nothing but sunshine. Tim checks the aviation-weather Web site for the weather at Valley City, fifty miles to the west. Clear there, too. So at 10:00 AM he says the flight is a go. The winds are from the southeast at 22 knots. The primary crew for this day, however, is already gone. A fixed-wing flight to Rochester. Jason has come in, simply because he knew he'd be called sooner or later, and has spent the morning with a computer flight simulator, learning to land a helicopter in Washington, D.C. Someone in the process has called Dwayne Chevalier, another flight paramedic, who is less than ten minutes away.

Jason picks up the phone and talks with the MeritCare emergency room to get more details. He learns the patient is a twenty-one-year-old woman who rolled her car a little after eight that morning. She managed to get herself out of the car, and then flagged someone down to take her to Valley City's Mercy Hospital emergency room. Bruises, maybe some minor fractures, is all they report. If it was just that, he tells me, no one would call the helicopter. But this woman is seven months pregnant. No signs of labor. But there is that risk.

Jason goes downstairs to the emergency room to get some type of fetal monitor while Tim and I go upstairs to the hangar. The hangar door goes up, the hoist lifts the 222, and Tim wheels it back onto the pad. Jason appears and stores some extra gear. I crawl in the back and watch Tim and Jason walk to the edge of the pad and look down to the street. Suddenly, they both wave and head back to the helicopter.

Dwayne's here? I ask.

No reason to start the engines until he is, Jason says.

The engines begin their deep hum, and the blades begin to turn again. Dwayne takes the seat up front next to Tim, and at 10:15 AM the helicopter is in the air.

Valley City is straight west of Fargo on Interstate 94. The GPS unit shows our course, but it's just as easy on a day like this to follow the highway. This time of the morning, there's hardly any traffic at all. Jason and Dwayne point out homes of relatives and people they know, and talk about home prices and remodeling projects. Tim chimes in with a comment about the healthy crosswind correction, which causes the helicopter to look as if it were flying somewhat sideways. Jason mentions the extra equipment on board. Outside the window, I see the farmers have not yet been in the fields for planting, though the snow is finally gone. The earth is turning a dry, light shade of brown.

Tim asks Dwayne to call Mercy Hospital and make sure the landing pad is clear. A woman's voice comes back on the radio, saying, "Yes, I've already done that." Tim gives her an ETA of ten minutes.

We come in over Valley City at 2,500 feet with an airspeed of 127 knots and a ground speed of 122. The town really does rest in a small valley carved by the Sheyenne River, and the impression from the air is like flying into something below the horizon. The winds can be tricky. We pass over the town and hospital, and then bank and turn back toward the east for our landing. People on the streets and in their cars stop to watch our approach.

Tim calls out obstructions near the landing zone (LZ). Tall trees. Light poles. He calls them ahead of us, then abeam, then behind. In short, he talks through the landing so everyone knows what he's doing, and we can call out if we see something he cannot. "Heavy dust," he says, just before we land.

At 10:43 AM our skids rest on the ground. Jason and Dwayne are out of the helicopter and into the building faster than I can get my seat belt unfastened.

I move around to the front seat, and Tim shuts down the helicopter.

Now you just sit here and wait? I ask.

This isn't a secure LZ, he says. I have to stay here. And even if I didn't have to, it makes good sense.

He points to a house next door. No fence, he says. Any kid could come running. Anyone could come to the helicopter from any direction here. I don't like this LZ at all. I wish they would take some of those trees out. They did take out some a while back, but those others are a problem. And that air-handling equipment they put in for the building is way too close. This doesn't meet FAA [Federal Aviation Administration] regulations at all.

There's no way of telling how long Jason and Dwayne will be inside. It all depends on what they find there. But this morning they are back fast, and Tim jumps out to help them load the woman into the back. She's on a backboard, and her head is braced. Her face shows neither pain nor worry, but the deep-fatigue look of someone who's given her body to the grace of others. Jason makes a bit of small talk before the engine noise gets too loud and comforts her.

This is going to be a nearly vertical takeoff, guys, Tim says. We lift off at 11:08 AM, and Tim calls out the obstructions again. The winds are a bit more from the south, and stronger now. It's at 27 knots, gusting to 33. Clear of the trees and lights and rising out of the valley, Tim lowers the nose a bit to gain forward speed, and we are heading back to Fargo and MeritCare.

The woman in back is simply resting. Something is itching her foot, she says, but that's about it. We watch the farms and roads pass underneath us. As we approach town, our path takes us within a mile of the south end of Hector Field, and this morning two F-16s from the North Dakota Air National Guard are coming in. The first one lands, full stop. The second one, however, does a touch-and-go. We listen as ATC tells him where and what we are. And we watch, as his course would bring him very close to us. But even before the end of the runway, the pilot of the F-16 stands the thing on end and rockets nearly straight up, a slight turn to the west thrown in for fun.

I was hoping he'd do that, Tim says.

At 11:30 AM we touch down at MeritCare, and the woman is taken downstairs to emergency. Tim refills the helicopter, seventy-five gallons to fly about 100 miles, and then rolls it back into the narrow hangar. By the time we get downstairs, Jason and Dwayne have already come back from emergency. She's fine, they say. A little bleeding, and maybe a small bone fracture. But nothing, really.

Still, Jason says, you'd hate to have it go the other way.

4. SEATS *and Heavies*

✶ ✶ ✶ ✶

Just south of Miles City, Montana, a white plume of smoke rises to the otherwise clear, bright sky. Late afternoon, mid-July, the fields and ranges are the brown of a hard, dry summer, and the temperature is approaching one hundred degrees. Traffic moves fast and easily over Interstate 94. But that plume is a problem. That plume is fire smoke, grass and timber, and the wind is up. The early clouds of a distant storm rest on the horizon. From the radio in my Jeep I know already that this storm will bring wind and dry lightning. Little rain, if any, will reach the ground.

Farther west, more plumes appear in every distance. The storm clouds grow larger. I watch the occasional lightning bolt jump from sky to ground. And then the brown cloud starts. I can see it in the northwest distance, tumbling over itself, ground level, heading for the highway. Thick and long, like the exhaust trail of some furnace, it reminds me of a narrow sandstorm, only denser, and more ominous. I am still fifty-three miles east of Billings, rising into some small pass in the hills, when I meet this cloud, and the wind that comes with it. And it is all I can do to keep my Jeep on the road. Seriously, I wonder if I will make it.

Whatever song is on the radio is interrupted by the harsh beeps of a weather alert. Severe thunderstorm warning. Winds in excess of seventy miles an hour. This storm already has a history of damaging winds, trees knocked down, buildings damaged. When the DJ comes back on, he lists off places that have power and those that do not. "This storm is wreaking havoc," he says. "Just wreaking havoc!"

In a folder on my passenger seat, I have a map from the NIFC, the National Interagency Fire Center in Boise, Idaho. Published every day, this map shows the location and name and size of every "large incident" fire in the United States. "Large incident" means a wildfire of one hundred acres or more in timber, or a wildfire of three hundred acres or more in grass and sage. And with this map I also have the daily situation report, which details every fire and nearly every resource thrown at it. The situation report tells me the names, the states, the size of each fire, the percentage contained, the number of people working it, the number of fire engines and helicopters, the number of structures lost. But the map and the situation report do not tell me what I really want to know. I want to know where the airplanes are.

We have all seen the pictures. Lockheed P2s and P3s, painted a dramatic red and white, or C-130s, diving low toward some fire, doors in the belly suddenly opening and red slurry falling away from the airplane, covering the ground, laying down a line of fire retardant the fire is not supposed to pass. And we've seen the videos of the accidents, the C-130 coming in for a run, its wings suddenly snapping upward, the fuselage nosing into the ground, all lives lost. And a lot of us have even seen the movie *Always*, the 1989 Steven Spielberg story with Richard Dreyfuss and Holly Hunter and Audrey Hepburn's last film appearance, a love story about the pilots who fight wildfires. But the pictures and the videos and movie say nothing, really, about the flying. What does it take, I wonder, to point a heavy air tanker toward a fire? What does it feel like when the chutes open and the load falls away? What does it take to fly a much smaller plane, a converted crop sprayer, into the same picture? All summer long, all over the country, there are pilots fighting fires. And I want to meet them.

Even though it's not on the situation report, there is a woman in Boise, Rose Davis, who knows where the planes are. Her full title is public affairs specialist, U.S. Department of Agriculture Forest Service, Fire and Aviation Management, National Interagency Fire Center. I've never met her, but we've been e-mailing for years, and she knows what I want to discover. Months ago I told her when I would be able to travel, and asked if she would point me toward the closest fire with the most flying. Two weeks ago, northern California caught fire, and that's where I thought I would be going. Then there were fires in Nevada. Then two days before I was set to leave, dry lighting hit Montana. Drought-stricken Montana. On the fire maps and the situation report, I watched the birth and growth of something called the Saunders Fire, just north of Billings. Is this a good place, I asked her? In an e-mail, she wrote, "You must have a lucky star following you, I tell you what. It's very difficult to have this many factors—active fire, both kinds of aircraft and likely flying activity—to all come together." So I pointed the Jeep west, toward Billings.

On the highway, however, I have serious questions about this lucky star. That brown cloud is not from the Saunders Fire. Whatever fire it's from is too new for the NIFC maps. Every moment that wind grows stronger and that cloud grows thicker. I am driving through a storm with seventy-mile-an-hour winds, and the sky behind me to the east turns charcoal gray. The sky to the north is a lighter gray, illuminated by the sun a little bit differently, but thick, heavy smoke blankets the highway, covers the ground. There is a peculiar smell to grass smoke versus wood smoke or charcoal, and I can feel the grasslands burning as that smell comes into the Jeep. On the cell phone with my wife, I tell her it feels like driving through an end-of-the-world scene.

Finally, then, Billings and the hotel. On the television, alerts and emergency interruptions fill the channels, harsh beeps and then fast white type on a black screen. These are not weather messages. Civil emergency, the text says. Yellowstone County

Disaster and Emergency Services has issued an alert. There is a new wildfire just north of Pompeys Pillar. Evacuations should begin immediately. Residents in the area east of Bundy Road, near Scothern Road, need to evacuate now.

I know Pompeys Pillar, that spot on the Yellowstone River where William Clark carved his name into the rock, the only physical evidence of the entire Corps of Discovery that remains on the trail. But I do not know Bundy Road, Scothern Road, or any of the other place-names the television announces. I do not know if the evacuations are small families leaving occasional farmsteads, or masses of people leaving tightly packed neighborhoods. I turn the sound down, though I still read the scrolling warnings, and sleep is difficult to find.

Day 1

The next day dawns clear and bright. There are some clouds in the distance, but not of any substance. The forecast is for a hot day, possibly some thunderstorms in the afternoon. None of them producing much rain. Fire risk is high. In the distance to the south, I can see the Beartooth mountain range. I've been there before, up the road through the Beartooth Pass and then into Yellowstone National Park, where they had their own fire not so many years ago. Dramatic and beautiful country. To the north and to the east of the airport, though, just buttes, valleys, flatland, brown earth. And two huge plumes of fire smoke rise on the far horizon.

At the Billings airport this morning, Logan International, two P3 Orion tankers wait outside the tanker base on the northeast side of the airport. The wings and the middle third of each plane are painted white. The front third and the tails are painted red. Black stripes separate the colors. On the tail of one tanker, the white number 22. On the tail of the other, 00. The four turboprop engines, each propeller holding four blades, are quiet.

Strong planes, I think. This is the same airframe NOAA uses for its version of the Hurricane Hunters.

A man named Don Smurthwaite meets me in the main Bureau of Land Management (BLM) office. Dark-haired and thin, he is the public affairs officer, and Rose has told him I'm coming. In an e-mail this morning she wrote, "Don left a message for me last night and he got dispatched to the fire which he described as pretty awesome. He is still planning on meeting you and everything, but he was quite wowed at the force of this particular incident and they are looking at more wind over the next two or three days."

"You were at the fire?" I ask him. "What were you doing?"

"Talking to the media," he says. "Answering questions from the public. That sort of thing. We got treated to quite an air show yesterday."

There is a briefing at the tanker base at 8:00 AM and we are a bit early, so Don runs me through a fast introduction. Allen Edmonds, the state aviation manager, essentially the boss of the whole operation, wears a checkered shirt, blue jeans, graying hair, and an easy smile. We shake hands, promise to catch up with each other when things get quieter. Then it's off to the tanker base a few yards away. Long, and about as wide as a mobile home, the inside is nothing fancy. Half of it is a rest area for the pilots and mechanics and loading crews, a kitchen space, a television, and some couches. The other half is taken up by one long table covered with papers and forms, handheld radios, and headsets. This is the work half. There are a few small offices off this space, and a bathroom, and there is a door that leads to a small deck between the building and the airport fence. There is a combination keypad on the outside doors, but the doors are propped open. Men and women walk in and out, many of them greeting each other like old friends after a long time apart—last fire season, I guess—and everyone in some sense is getting ready.

Don introduces me to Michele Hodik, a woman in her early twenties with short brown hair, one of the ramp managers, who gives me a quick primer on the workings of a tanker base. The fire retardant, sometimes called slurry, sometimes called mud, officially called Phos-Check, arrives by semitruck outside the tanker base. Ammonium polyphosphate, which slows fire even after the water in it has evaporated, mixed with corrosion inhibitor and iron oxide for color, it's off-loaded into three steel tanks next to the building, each tank holding 10,000 gallons of unmixed retardant. A fourth tank, 5,000 gallons, holds just water for mixing. It's pumped by the retardant and then stored briefly in a fifth tank, also 5,000 gallons, for the mixed solution. Nine thousand gallons at a time, the semis have been coming every other day since there's been so much flying.

Outside the tanks, pumps and hoses and valves create the paths for the retardant to reach two loading pits on the ramp. Hoses run from a fire hydrant to the water tank, and also up to each pit. Pit 1, right outside the tanker base, is for the converted crop sprayers, the single-engine air tankers, or SEATS, whereas Pit 2, a bit farther away to the left, is for the Heavies. The two P3s are the Heavies, while a third, a P2 Neptune, Tanker 10, is across the field at the Edwards Jet Center with a mechanical problem.

"That plane should be back this morning," Michele tells me. "At least we hope so."

The mixture is 4.75 gallons of water to each gallon of retardant, and Tankers 00 and 22 each hold 2,500 gallons of mixed slurry. A gallon of straight retardant weighs 9 pounds. A gallon of the mix weighs 12 pounds. Thirty thousand pounds of retardant dropped every time the plane makes a run.

Loading a Heavy takes about ten to fifteen minutes. The SEATS hold only 500 or 800 gallons, though, depending on the plane, so that job is much quicker. Five minutes if everything is going well. Ten minutes if the process goes badly.

It's a confusing dance at times. The two P3s are owned by a

company called AeroUnion, based in Chico, California. Tanker 10, the P2, is owned by Neptune Aviation, based in Missoula, Montana. The SEATS are owned by a company called New Frontier, based in Fort Benton, Montana. Each of the Heavies has its own crew and its own mechanics. The SEATS bring their own loading crews as well. Add a handful of government agencies, I think, and the whole thing tends toward chaos. But no, Michele says, the place works pretty well.

"You know," she says, "this is my first summer here."

"You're kidding," I say. "Exciting so far?"

"Yeah. But I'd rather be out on the fire line," she says. "I just want to be where there's more action. That's where you cut your teeth."

* * *

8:35 AM. Everyone gathers on the deck at the tanker base. Some people sit at the wooden tables; others sit on the railing. A good many just stand. All told, there must be twenty-five or thirty people.

On the other side of the fence, Heavy Tankers 00 and 22 and SEATS 407, 472, and 464 are parked and ready. An Aerocommander, a twin-engine, high-wing airplane, and a Beechcraft 90 wait beyond them. A Cessna 182 is also nearby. And over by a hangar, Tanker 59, the B-26 used in the movie *Always*.

Sitting on the rail, Michele begins the briefing with a weather report. Red-flag warning, she says. A hot day coming. More dry lightning in the afternoon. She lists specific forecasts for specific locations, and I can see people nod, as if saying, "Yep, that's where I'll be." Then it's Bob Flesch's turn. Bob is the unit aviation manager, basically the guy in charge of operations. Sitting on the rail next to Michele, Bob is tall and thin, wears a baseball cap, has a goatee that's grown a bit long, and speaks with a soft voice. He quickly turns the meeting over to Kelly Elder, a seasonal aircraft dispatcher who works for the Helena Interagency Dispatch Center but has come to Billings to help.

"We've got orders for Pine Ridge as well as Bundy Railroad," Kelly says. "I think maybe we'll tie in with Bob and figure it out how that's going to happen here right after the briefing. The thought is to keep the two Heavies in tandem with one another. We'll co-ordinate the airspace such as that we've got a Lead with the two Heavies, and maybe the Air Attack over the other incident with SEATS. I don't know. Bob, we'll talk. But for frequencies, folks, I realize there was a lot of traffic yesterday. I really apologize. I know people outside the area were a little frustrated with us. To help that out, today there are frequencies for the Bundy Railroad. We did get those frequencies, air to air and air to ground. We've also requested new frequencies for Pine Ridge. We just placed those this morning, so I don't know when those will come through. We have asked for an air to air and air to ground on Pine Ridge as well. That might help with congestion there. You can't request TFR [temporary flight restriction] until you have your frequencies—your air-to-air and air-to-ground frequencies. Those were taking about a three-and-a-half-hour turnaround to go through Boise yesterday. I know it's a concern of yours. I was trying to work on it. The Bundy Railroad fire TFR probably didn't come out till five hours after Initial Attack. It was a priority from minute 1. Bob came in and said, 'You're on that, right?' I said, 'Yeah, I'm on it.' We're doing the best we can do with TFRs."

Two fire groups in the eastern distance. One called Bundy Railroad. The other called Pine Ridge. Both appear on the NIFC fire maps today.

Bob tells everyone it's going to be a busy morning, and asks if there are any questions. This morning, there are none.

* * *

There is no whistle. No siren blows, and no one goes running to his airplane. But after the briefing the tanker base is in a different gear. There is more urgency in the way people move. It's like listening to a long crescendo. It builds and builds, and you just know at some point it's going to erupt. Allen walks by the pumps, out into the parking lot, back to the pumps, then out to the ramp, a cell phone pinned to his ear. Bob walks by one way with a stack of papers, then walks the other way with a stack twice as large.

The Beechcraft is the first airplane to start its engines. Tanker 22 is connected to the hoses in Pit 2 and pumped full of mud. And then the show begins in earnest.

9:05 AM. Tanker 22 begins to fire up its engines, the high whine of the starter followed by the deep air rush when the fuel in the turbines begins to burn. Allen runs out to the ramp to give the hand signals to the pilot.

9:17 AM. Tanker 00 starts its engines, taxis to Pit 2, and is loaded with retardant. At the same time, the Cessna 182 and the three SEATS come to life, one right after the other. As they begin to taxi, I can hear the sound of a feathered prop being turned so the blades bite air.

9:24 AM. Tanker 00 rolls away from the ramp. Jim Hassler, the senior ramp manager, gives the signals to send it off. The three SEATS line up at Pit 1 for their loads. SEAT 407 is first. Loading crews pull the hoses, attach them to the plane, talk on their radios to the crew down by the tanks and pumps. When the plane is full, the hoses are disconnected, and red spray splatters the crew and the ground.

9:26 AM. SEAT 407 leaves, and SEAT 464 pulls up. SEAT 464 is a pretty plane, the same white and red as the others, tanker numbers in block letters on the tail, but whereas 407 and 472 are turboprops, long-nosed and sleek, faster and more powerful, 464 has the old-style radial engine, the piston cylinders going around in a circle behind the prop. It's a new airplane, built in Europe, but everything about it speaks to an older time.

9:29 AM. SEAT 464 taxis away toward the runway. SEAT 472

pulls up to the pit. Almost identical to 407, 472, however, is also a trainer, a two-seater. A Canadian registration number is painted on the side.

When 464 leaves, there is a moment when the world seems to relax. No engine noise. No sound of props moving forward. Michele hoses spilled retardant off a loading pit and into a drain. Allen sits on a pump near the tanks and lights a cigar. Jim fusses with some equipment. Between the tanker base and the BLM building, a man on a riding mower and a woman with a weed-eater greet each other as they pass. It could be any soft summer morning on the edge of the Rockies. But in the eastern distance, the plumes are larger than they were before.

10:00 AM. Suddenly, Tanker 22 is back at Pit 2 for reloading. It's not that the plane is that fast. The fires are simply that close. The plumes on the horizon are growing fast. The SEATS are coming back, too. SEAT 407 is the first to pull up to Pit 1. Then Tanker 00 is on the ramp, waiting for the pit to clear.

10:06 AM. Tanker 22 leaves again. Around the SEATS and the Heavies, normal air traffic continues at the airport. Jets for United and Big Sky Aviation carry passengers wherever they're going or bring them to Billings, and I wonder what those passengers think when they look out the window and see the red and white tankers.

10:10 AM and there is a problem with Pit 2. Jim and the loading crew connect the hoses and the pumps are turned on, but nothing goes. Something is clogging the hoses that pump slurry from the holding tanks to the pit. Tanker 00 waits on the ramp for the SEATS to clear, and then the crew disconnects the hoses, the engines fire up, and the tanker moves to Pit 1. When it's finally done, Tanker 22 is already back again, wheels touching down on the runway.

There are multiple fires on the horizon now. Standing here at the airport, I count one, two, three, four, five, six plumes in what I think is the Bundy Railroad complex. Slightly more off to the south, a mass of billowing clouds makes it impossible to count the individual fires at Pine Ridge. And silhouetted against the smoke, the small shapes of Tanker 00 heading out, the SEATS heading in.

* * *

Sometimes, complex systems are the best evidence for evolution. You would never design the current process for fighting fires with airplanes if you started with blank paper in a quiet room. It doesn't make easy sense. It doesn't look efficient. But fires are not easy, and their progress can change as whimsically as a breeze. So over time, one fire at a time, the methods worked themselves out.

It begins, as it should, with a firefighter on the ground. His team needs more than their sweat and their Pulaskis and their fire trucks can offer. So he calls the dispatch room at the BLM building and requests a tanker. In the dispatch room, there are dispatchers for equipment, dispatchers for personnel, people who follow the staging of materials and forecast where to stage them next. The whole dance moves through here. And if the request is granted, dispatch calls the tanker base and the aviation process starts.

First off the ground is a plane they call the Air Attack. Here in Billings, that plane is the Aerocommander or the Cessna, both with high wings for best downward visibility. Air Attack has a pilot to keep the plane in the sky, and a firefighter to observe the ground. Once on-site, Air Attack talks on the radio with the crews on the ground to identify drop sites and obstructions, discuss needs and priorities, and lay out the plan for the tankers. Then comes the Lead plane, the Beech 90. The Lead plane gets instructions from Air Attack, and then flies the routes they want the tankers to take. Lead scouts the drop run, looks for exit places, looks for exit places if an engine fails, thinks its way through all the possible problems, and then waits for the tankers.

Twelve miles away from the fire, the tankers call Air Attack and are either invited into the area or told to hold. When Air Attack has the ground crew ready and other airplanes where they need to be, the tankers are brought in. Lead circles and waits, the three planes talk about landmarks and procedures, and when the timing is right Lead turns toward the run and the tanker follows closely behind. It's a game of chase, or follow me. The tanker drops its load of retardant and heads back to the tanker base, but Lead and Air Attack stay on-site as long as fuel allows, evaluate the drop, plan the next rush with the crew on the ground.

Then some other ground crew calls dispatch for their own need. Some crew fighting a fire two states away needs a Heavy to keep their fire contained. A power line is threatened, but so is a barn, or a house, or livestock in some ravine. Decisions start to get difficult. Air traffic control is slow to establish a TFR, so there are stray airplanes in the fire zone. There are air-to-air, as well as air-to-ground, radio frequencies to be set up so the crews and Air Attack and Lead and Heavies and SEATS can all talk, without being confused with or by the other fires in radio range. And then there are problems with the hoses pumping retardant to Pit 1. Allen Edmonds paces the parking lot with a cell phone to his ear. Bob Flesch never sits down.

*   *   *

Inside the tanker base, the center of gravity is the long table. And at the center of the table, Tory Snedigar keeps the world in order. Thirty years old, long brown hair, married with small children, she's the one person with an ear to everything. On the table in front of her, stacks of dispatch sheets show destinations for the airplanes, frequencies, latitude and longitude. Stacks of time cards for each airplane, which she punches into a time-stamp machine, keep track of flying time. SEATS and Heavies are paid a daily fee for being available, and an additional rate for flight time. Plus, no pilot can fly more than eight hours a day. There are maps and TFR announcements, three-hole punches, aircraft reports, as well as the stuff everyone from the outside sets down to look at something else. Hats. Radios. Food wrappers. Three or four pairs of sunglasses. Coffee cups. Water bottles.

Behind her, a small desk in front of a window that looks out toward Pit 2 holds a computer and a telephone, a radio to talk with people and planes on the ramp, another radio that listens to the conversation between Air Attack and Billings dispatch. Looking out the window, I can see Jim in his bright-orange shirt, Michele in a reflective vest, and other people getting ready to load a plane. The sky is clear. The temperature is already more than ninety degrees.

"Can I get the water on here at Pit 2?" Michele's voice is loud over the ramp radio. Then Jim's voice comes through equally strong as a SEAT pulls up. "Welcome to the ramp!" he cries. When the plane stops rolling, Tory keys her mike and says, "407, in the blocks at 10:58." She puts the time card for 407 in the machine and stamps it.

"10:58," the pilot replies.

On the smaller radio, One Bravo Gulf, the Air Attack plane, is talking to dispatch about diverting planes from one fire to the other. Tory gets on the ramp radio again.

"407, hold after you're done loading. We may have a new assignment for you."

A few seconds later, the telephone rings. Someone in the dispatch office is calling Tory with the new assignments. She fills out the sheet, then asks whoever is standing nearby to run the paper out to the pilot.

"I am listening," she tells me. "I can pretty much tell what's going to happen. But I do have to wait for the phone call, for the official word."

A few moments later, filled with slurry and now heading somewhere new, 407 gets clearance from the Billings tower and calls Tory again.

"407 rolling," the pilot says.

Tory puts the time card in the machine again and radios the pilot.

"407, rolling at 11:13."

A new worry had crept into the tanker base. The fires are so close, and so big, the SEATS and Heavies are already on their fourth loads. The tanker base is racing through retardant, and what's in the tanks outside may not last the day. One of the truckers bringing new retardant calls and says she won't be here until after 6 PM.

"Are you going to make it?" I ask Tory.

"We'll see," she says.

The news gets around that the TFRs have been put in place. Frequencies changed. And now planes are being diverted to the Pine Ridge fires from the other complexes. Structures are threatened. A big plate of store-bought M&M cookies is put on the long table, and stressed people smile when they take one.

Bob Flesch walks through the room, and Tory calls to him. "Are the SEATS doing okay in the wind?" she asks.

"It's steady," he replies, heading into his office. He is followed by a woman who looks decidedly unhappy.

"She's from over in dispatch," Tory says to me quietly. "And she's always unhappy."

Two more SEATS show up, and again Jim's voice booms from the radio through the base. "Welcome to the ramp!"

"Are you having fun?" I ask Tory.

Her eyes grow bright at the question. "You should ask Jim that question," she laughs to me. And a few minutes later, when Jim comes into the building, grabs a cookie, and drops down into a chair, I ask him exactly that.

"Living the dream, my friend," he says to me. "Living the dream."

* * *

1:10 in the afternoon. I drive away from the airport and down the hill into Billings for a few minutes, just to grab some lunch, and when I turn the Jeep back toward the ridge I nearly drive off the road. Thick white smoke is pouring over the ridgetop. My first thought is that some plane has crashed, but the smoke is the wrong color, and there is too much of it. This is grassland fire smoke. But clearly something new has happened.

When I get back to the base, I see a new fire has broken out less than a mile away from the airport. Tory tells me there was a fire there last night, and a crew was still there, working to put out the smoldering hot spots. "But with this wind," she says, "it just came back to life." And the wind continues to get stronger. In the distance, at least from what I can tell, Bundy Railroad and Pine Ridge continue to grow. So the planes continue to fly.

Tankers 00 and 22 are both on the ground, as well as a SEAT. On the ramp radio, Jim is yelling to the men at the tanks and pumps to shut one of the pumps down. But the men at the pumps can't hear him. Michele and Tory both go running outside, waving.

One of the Heavies, Tanker 00, is going to hit this fire right behind us. "It's already jumped a ridge and getting pretty big," Tory says.

On the ramp radio, Tory gives the pilot the assignment and tells him they don't have a bearing for it. "But once you get in the air, you should be able to see it," she says.

He says, "Yeah, it's tough to miss this one."

The Lead plane is already overhead when Tanker 00 begins to roll down the runway. Once it's in the air, the tanker begins a slow climbing turn to the right, and the Beech makes its own right turns over the fire. The tanker meets up with the Lead, and I swear it looks like ballet. One turn around the fire, then another, the two planes slowly descend with each circuit. Then on some signal the Beech turns more sharply and cuts in front of the much larger Tanker. Both dive toward the smoke and fire.

I am watching this from a walkway on top of the retardant tanks, and suddenly Don Smurthwaite is on the ground below me. "You certainly don't get to see this every day!" he calls.

The white Lead races over the smoke and pulls up. The red and white tanker dives low behind it, nearly to the horizon of the ridge between us, and I can see the explosion of red slurry erupt from the plane. The smoke rising from the fire is immediately less.

Tanker 00 enters the airport traffic pattern to land and get another load of mud. The Lead plane heads off toward the other fires. Looking down into the open top of one of the retardant tanks, I can see that it is almost empty.

* * *

2:25 in the afternoon and Tanker 10 rumbles over to the tanker base from Edwards Jet Center, where it's been finishing up repairs. Something wrong with one of its cylinders, I've been told. And everything that could go wrong with the repair did go wrong. But now it's ready. Tanker 10 is a Lockheed P2 Neptune, much older than Tankers 00 and 22, the much larger Lockheed P3 Orions. At 91 feet, 8 inches long, with a wingspan of 103 feet, 10 inches, Tanker 10 has two large piston-driven engines, one on each wing, each rated at 3,750 shaft horsepower, as well as two jets, rated at 3,400 pounds of static thrust. This is the model that was built to replace the B-17 and the B-24, with a larger bomb bay that now holds fire retardant, and lived its life between World War II and Vietnam, hunting submarines. It has a glass bubble for a nose. The tail is red, with a white number 10, and the top of the plane is white, while the wings and the bottom are silver. There is a lightning bolt up the side. Like the old Flying Tigers, the jets are painted with teeth.

"Welcome to the ramp!" Jim calls through the radio, and nearly everyone at the tanker base is smiling. There is another Heavy in Billings.

It's 2:55 in the afternoon when Tanker 10 starts its roll down the runway for the first time today. Dispatch calls Tory, who then tells Tanker 22 to hold after loading. They're going to switch his assignment to the town of Ashland. "So I guess we're not going to save the power lines anymore," the pilot radios back. "It's power lines or Ashland," Tory replies.

On the flight-following radio, I hear Air Attack and dispatch give the same order I've heard all morning. When a Heavy or a SEAT heads back to Billings, they're told to load and return. Load and return. Get some more mud, and get back here fast.

The phone line rings again. "Tanker base, Tory," she says. She listens and then shakes her head. "The retardant is still two and a half to three hours away," she says.

On the ramp, the heat is killing the radios. Batteries are dying, push-to-talk buttons are getting jammed in a permanent-transmit position. The planes cannot talk to the ground crews. The crews cannot talk to the people at the pumps. Tory can talk with the pilots, but not Jim or Michele or anyone else on the ground.

* * *

People are starting to ask about time. Pilots are limited to eight flying hours a day, and no one has taken a break. When the lunches arrived, they were carried out to the pilots, who ate them fast while the crews loaded slurry. No one has come in to take a break, or even go to the bathroom. Tory begins to add up the time cards.

"Tanker 22 is done," she says. "He's on his seventh load. Tanker 10 is just leaving with his third load, so he'll fly until pumpkin time."

"Pumpkin time?" I ask.

"Half an hour after legal sunset," she says. "The rules say you can't fly after that. Today that's 21:33. 9:33 PM."

She continues to add up the time, correcting mistakes as she goes along.

"Tanker 00 has seven loads, but he'll go back with an eighth. And let's see, our SEATS have done: 407 has eight. Eight for 472. 464 is a little slower, so he has seven."

It's 3:40 in the afternoon. The pilots are almost out of flying time, and the base is almost out of retardant. I walk outside and around the building so I can get a view of the eastern horizon. And as far as I can tell, it's one giant wall of smoke.

* * *

A man walks in from the ramp and settles heavily into one of the chairs at the long table. There's only a sliver of one of the cookies left.

"How is it out there?" I ask.

He pauses and sighs. "Job security," he says.

His name is Jeff Piechura. He's one of the firefighters in the Air Attack plane.

"Tell me how you do that?" I ask. "How do you sit up there and make sense of anything?"

"We're trying to get all the information as to who's on the fire, aerialwise. We're trying to define who's on the ground, what important priorities are relative to flight resources. Once we figure out who's there, it's just a matter of balancing who comes in first and how we get them in, and keep the helicopters and fixed wings separated so there aren't any problems."

"You're basically choreographing the dance," I say.

"Yes, that's fair."

"And you had helicopters there today too? They're not coming from here."

"We actually had one helicopter. We had that for about two hours. They were pulled off for a fire just north of the airport."

"They were just dipping a bucket somewhere and bringing it in?"

"Yeah, they were pulling it out of the river."

SEAT 407 calls in that it's rolling, and Tory radios back the time.

"How long have you been flying?" I ask.

"'94," he says. "I worked with the Fire Service, Northwest Fire District, in Tucson, Arizona. We flew a helicopter out of there. I've been doing helicopter work for about twenty years. Then I did Air Attack when my knees thought they couldn't take that anymore."

"And now?"

"I'm a firefighter—this is what I do. I listen to the radios, make sure that we're keeping separation in that aircraft coming in aren't at the same altitude as we are. Timing it such so that when the air tankers drop, I have a good view of it. It's not just spinning circles in the air; it's part of the dance, like you were saying—the choreograph."

"The reason you need a good view of it is to order the placement of the next drop or . . . ?"

"It's, one, to determine if the drop was good. It's an evaluation process and then lining up the next flight. Two, if there were a problem with the drop, then we can witness what that problem was."

In the background, Jim is on the ramp radio, trying to get his radio to work. "Tanker 407," he says, "how do you copy this?" There is no reply. Tory looks up through the window and keys her microphone. "You're clear, Jim." Then the SEAT is on the radio too. "407. Heard you loud and clear, Jim."

"Is it any good out there today?" I ask Jeff.

"The winds are just really pushing the fire," he says. "Up on top, we were being pushed by about 30-knot winds. On the ground, I imagine they're about 20–25."

"Are most of the drops good ones?"

Jeff smiles broadly and looks at my tape recorder.

"Nine out of ten drops are generally really good. Sometimes it's communications, either from the Air Attacks to the pilot that doesn't work out right, or we're picking out different landmarks when we're talking. Nine out of ten drops are really good."

I ask Jeff to tell me a story, a fire story or a flying story, one that he'll tell his grandkids first, and when he pauses several other people at the long table erupt into laugher. "Now you know he's not a pilot," someone says. "If he was a pilot he'd have a story, whether it was true or not." Someone behind me says, "Usually there's a girl involved. Or there was a rescue somewhere." Jeff just shakes it off.

"I've seen instances," he says, "where a fire just has its way with Mother Nature. We just have to sit back and watch how it wants to handle it. It's a sense of inferiority. Just kind of hanging back and watching the power of fire take over the land. It's truly the animal. It consumes, it breathes, it has waste, it digests. When it's done, we come in and take care of it. It's just awe-inspiring to watch it. Oh, sure, every firefighter wants to go in and beat it. You're hoping that the odds are going to swing in your favor with the weather and fuels and topography and stuff. You're betting on the combat. You've got resources coming that can make your next move successful. But today it's on the ground. The winds changed. It just didn't work out."

"Are we at least breaking even today?" I ask.

"No. Everything that we've dropped this morning is burned over. The winds pushed it over the top. This afternoon, we'll see. We're starting a defensive line now. We'll see how that holds."

* * *

5:23 PM. Listening to Air Attack talk to dispatch on the flight-following radio, we hear that homes are burning. The fire is already down to the Yellowstone River. They're pumping the river to try to save new homes. "She's a roamer, and she ain't stopping. This is going to be our big one," Tory says.

5:30 PM and SEAT 464 asks for total flying time. He's at more than six, which is rounded up to seven hours. He says, "Roger, I've got a couple more trips left in me."

With the heat and with the sunlight, this is a tremendously taxing day. And the fire is winning. So I am surprised when families, friends, and children show up to see the action. One little girl asks to touch the red stuff. Former employees show up just to hang out, to see what's going on. But from the porch at the tanker base, I can see why people want to be here. It's exciting as all hell. The planes show up, and the pit crews move like they are in a race, which of course they are. There is the noise of the airplane engines, the props as they feather. There is the dramatic site of the red-and-white paint jobs. There is the beauty of an airplane rolling down a runway and then lifting off into the sky. Unless you're listening to an air-traffic radio, there's no way to know what's happening in the distance.

I am talking with Michele and a man named Nathan Hall, the junior mechanic for Tanker 10, when the semitruck pulling a load of retardant shows up. Michele goes to help off-load the truck while a friend of Nathan's father shows up, so Nathan walks him out to the ramp for a tour of the plane.

Tanker 00 is set to leave for its last load of the day, and on the ramp radio Jim tells the crew to park on the other side of the airport, at Edwards Jet Center, when they return.

"If I don't see you," he says, "you're doing a great job. We appreciate everything."

"Thank you very much," the pilot responds. "It's our pleasure."

Someone reports that there are forty or fifty cars over at the airport observation area, people standing with their hands against the chain-link fence.

In the background of the rest of the radios, we hear from dispatch an update that at one location, three hundred head of cattle are threatened.

6:23 PM SEAT 464 times out for the day.

* * *

Matt Lutz is the pilot of SEAT 464. From Lewistown, Montana, young and dark-haired with a Hollywood smile, he's already been here a week, flying on fires. SEAT 464 is the radial-engine SEAT, an M-18 Dromader, a plane built in Poland. Its tank holds 500 gallons.

"Yeah, it was hard," he tells me. "The wind kept switching. It just kept going around the line. Finally, it was just a matter of structure protection. That's what we're doing right now. Those guys are just down burning the head. It's kinda got two heads now, and it's all the way down to the river. It's a mess. It will probably cross the river and join up with that other one on the south side."

"They're that close right now?" I ask.

"Well, I'd say ten, fifteen miles. I'd say that railroad fire ran at least fifteen miles last night. I don't know how many miles it ran today, but it's rolling."

"Walk me through one of your flights?" I ask.

"We contact Air Attack or the Lead twelve miles out and establish radio communication with him," he says. "Once we have communication with him, we've got to close the door with Billings dispatch, and then that's just one less thing to worry about. Air Attack gives us an altimeter setting and an altitude to come in. We have to have a clearance from him. It's nice, because if there's more airplanes as you're coming in, he'll direct you in at a certain altitude. Then, you can kind of watch what's going on in most cases. He'll just explain: 'Just hook on and tie on to that last drop,' or 'See that last drop?' He can kind of direct you from there. But there's nothing you can really do about it. These little airplanes are made for Initial Attacks. These big fires, I mean, yeah, we can do structure protection and fill in the gaps with the Heavies, but other than that, it's just a long shot. I guess you've got to try to do something."

"Do the SEATs use the Lead plane the same way that the Heavies do?"

"Well, if the Lead plane's available, we'll use it. If not, more than most, no, we don't use the Lead plane. Since the Heavies are in the same mix, the Lead plane is there. So he'll go down and give us a show-me. We use them more as a show-me, rather than a Lead because of the vortices. We don't want to get into their wake. He's talking to Air Attack all the time. They coordinate together. Just following him, it makes it real easy."

"What was it like flying today?"

"It was miserable."

"Just hot?"

"Yeah. And rough. Landings were quartering cross. It was like 30 knots. There were a bunch of wind-shear warnings."

"Can you tell me a fire story?" I ask.

Matt gets a huge smile on his face, and pauses. Then he goes on.

"It is pretty interesting. I just try to be safe. If I don't like it, I don't do it. It's as dangerous as you make it, I guess, is a good way to put it."

"Where are you guys, above ground level, on a drop?"

"Well, we're supposed to stay above sixty feet on the job. That is fairly low."

"Sixty feet is about where you hit it every time?"

"Yeah, sixty. Or a little lower probably."

"What's it like when you drop a load? You lose a lot of weight all of a sudden."

"Yeah, but you compensate for that. I usually have the nose trimmed way down, and I'm pulling back on the stick when I drop. When the load goes, the nose just comes right up."

"Do you see a lot of the ground crews as you drop?"

"A lot of times, it's hard to get them out of the way."

We both pause and look at the people standing around the desk, the loading crews at the pits, the clear and cloudless sky.

"Is it working at all today?" I ask.

"I don't know."

* * *

In the blocks.

Rolling.

Load and return.

The radio cadence continues.

The cooler by the television is out of bottled water, and someone brings in several new cases from somewhere outside. Dinners of fried chicken show up in bags for the pilots and mechanics, the loaders and the office people. There is no ceremony or gathering. People grab a meal as they can. Jim comes in, and then Michele, then several of the loaders. The planes that are on the ramp are all done for the day. Tanker 10 is still flying; SEATS 407 and 472 are close to timing out.

Kevin Meekin has been the pilot of the Lead plane today. Close black hair and dark sunglasses, this is the guy who could get away with wearing a white silk aviator's scarf. He comes into the base, drinks two bottles of water, sits at the kitchen counter, and eats one of the dinners, not really talking to anyone. But no one is talking much. On the evening of a hot day, there is a moment when the air temperature falls below body temperature, and it feels like you've been storing heat all day. It starts to come out of your skin, under your hair, around your ears, inside your shoes.

"When you have a moment," I say.

He nods at me. He finishes his meal, drinks another bottle of water, comes to the long table with logbooks and paperwork.

When he's done, we go outside, pass Allen and Bob talking in the parking lot, and find two chairs on the other deck, the one on the east side of the building, now in cool shadow. In the distance, we can see the massive plumes of the fires.

"So what were you doing before you were doing this?" I ask, smiling.

"Flying freight," he laughs. "Actually, I was flying one of those 99s sitting over there."

"You saw this and you said, 'I want to get over there'?"

"Yeah, I had flown Air Attack before in a previous job—you know, I was the Air Attack pilot. I had a little exposure to it to start with."

"So tell me about flying the Lead plane," I say. "I know that your job is to basically chart the path for the drop. Right? To show the pilot, the tankers, the Heavies, or the SEATS. But what are you actually telling them?"

"We're showing them where the drop is. Where to start; where to stop. We're down there looking for, you know, we'll go fly it first before the tanker ever shows up. We're looking for obstructions, visibility, smoke and everything to actually get in there. We're looking for the exit, where they're going to go after the drop. We're going to look for the exit, where they're going to go if they lose an engine down there or have some kind of mechanical problems. Looking, checking the air for turbulence, seeing how rough it is."

"So, when you make your first pass, you go through so high and then just do several passes to get lower?"

"Yeah, that's what you do. When you show up on-scene, you're either talking to the Air Attack or the ground contact to see kind of what their plan is. You're working with them to figure out—are we going to go down the right flank or the left flank, across header, or whatever. Then, once we get that figured out, I'll start looking and seeing what or how we're actually going to go down that flank and decide whether we're going to start up on this end, go down, or which end to go the other way. While I'm doing that, you're up fairly high still."

"AGL, what would you be?" I ask, curious as to his distance above ground level.

"A thousand. So we're getting the big picture. You know, the way the drainage is laid and everything. You're looking for any obstructions, towers, and power lines."

"I saw a map on one of the walls inside," I say. "A firefighter-pilot hazard map of some sort. Are they pretty good?"

"Well," he chuckles, "they get you started in the right direction. I'm not going to rely on that. Let's put it this way, I won't get out there on-site and not survey and see what's out there. At the same time, I'm looking for the drainages, where's lowering terrain. You always want to do the drops into lowering terrain. You don't want to go into a blind canyon, of course. Once I get that pretty well figured out, then I'll start working my way down to where I'm actually making the run at a 150-feet AGL.

"So your run is going to be at the same altitude as the drop. The SEATS go in at 60 feet. But the Heavies go in at 150?"

"Yeah, at 150 is their minimum drop. It will be like 150 to 200 feet is what they drop at."

"How do you communicate to the Heavies? 'Here's not only the run I want you to do, but here's the exit if you have a problem. Here's the exit if you don't.'"

"You just tell them on the radio. That's part of the direction. When they show up, you give them first an incoming briefing—give them the altimeter. What altitude you want them coming into the fire. What altitude you're at. What altitude the air tanker is at and any other aircraft in the fire. Usually, we tell them what load we're going to launch—a full load, a half load. And what coverage level. As they come in, we'll start pointing out the run to them. That's when we're going to be telling them where the exit is, where they're going to go and where I'm going to go. Just so they know. You know, I want to get out of their way."

"Aren't you faster than they are?"

"I still want to get out of their way," he laughs.

7:12 in the evening and the second semitruck of retardant shows up.

"We don't just have one run planned out for the tankers if you're doing your job right," he continues, "because with all these fires today, the wind is out of the west one minute; two minutes later it's out of the north. You're always trying to have a couple different runs planned out. If the tanker shows up and can't do one run because it's all smoked in, we'll just go to plan B. We've got it all planned out and ready to go. That way you're not sitting there wasting time at six thousand dollars an hour."

"Did you fly the Lead for the drop right here? Was that you?"

"Yeah."

"I'm hearing today that it's a losing battle."

"The fire definitely has the upper hand on us, yeah."

"Can you tell me about Ashland? Were you part of those drops?"

"Yeah, I went down there."

"Did I hear right? They were dropping retardant in downtown Ashland?"

"Yeah, we made two SEAT drops right in downtown Ashland."

"You don't drop on the fire, so what were you doing?"

"We were there. There was a really hot spot. There were houses around it. There was a road there and a river on one side. There were structure fires. They wanted to cool it down. They had engines all the way around it. They just wanted to cool it down and take some of the steam out of it and just kind of slow it down. We dropped two SEAT loads right on the fire. That kind of took a little bit of the steam out of it."

"How about the other fires?" I ask.

"The problem there is, if you had five or six tankers lined up all ready to go, you could really get something done. When you drop one or two tankers, then you've got to wait for an hour to come back; everything's totally different. It's like starting all over again. But it does feel good when you actually save somebody's house from burning down."

"Do you ever have people coming up and saying, 'You saved my home'?"

"Oh, yeah. It makes you feel good. One of the benefits, I guess."

"Did it ever make you tremendously sad? When you fly over the house you didn't save?"

"You know, it bothers you. But when it comes right down to it, it's just a house. Nobody got killed. People have got to realize that, if they're going to live in the middle of the forest, that risk is there. You see so many houses that haven't done any fire prevention. People, what are you thinking? Then, you see other people do a really nice job in clearing the fields around their house. It's still a bummer when somebody's house burns down. It's going to happen sometimes, so you can't let it bother you. As long as nobody gets—you know. It does seem like a shame. There's a real nice house out on the bluff overlooking the Yellowstone River on the Saunders Fire a couple of days ago. We were going to try to put some retardant on it to help protect it. The first tanker was forty-five minutes away. By the time we got there, it was too late. Yeah, it was a nice house. That's what happens, I guess."

* * *

Joe Woolslayer is the pilot of SEAT 407. A bit older than the others, light-haired, the kind of person who grins more than smiles, he's timed out, finished the paperwork, and walked out to join us on the east-facing porch as the light begins to fade and Kevin has to leave.

"It's a losing battle today?" I ask.

"It's frustrating because we're not able to really affect the size of the fire or slow down the fire itself. But we have saved a lot of structures. We've saved a lot of property."

"I heard you talking on the radio," I said. "There's a story about some guy and his hay?"

Joe shakes his head. "Well," he says, "there was a house that was threatened. We put retardant all the way around it. The fire burned up to the retardant. But I guess the embers from the fire ignited the hay that was next to his house. Big, round hay bales. This guy had them right up next to the house. It was a huge fire. They were fighting it themselves on the ground. I left before I could see what was going to happen. He could lose his house because the hay is there."

"You didn't get a chance to go back?"

"No, I was out of time. We're only allowed to fly eight hours. Tanker 10 is still running, so he may get that put out."

On the horizon, the setting sun has turned the smoke plumes blue and pink. It is almost pretty.

"How did you get into this kind of flying?" I ask.

"I started out as a crop-duster pilot when I was seventeen years old, actually. That was in 1979 in Haskell, Oklahoma. I flew crop dusters for twenty-two years. Crop dusting got progressively terrible because of farming and different other reasons. For one thing, crop-dusting companies use these big airplanes now. They used to use more little airplanes, so there were more pilot positions. It paid better. So, crop dusting, basically, started getting bad. I got 'hold of a friend of mine, who was using these planes to fight fires. He said just come fly these. It pays real good. It's government work. That's how I did it. It's just kind of . . ."

"You had your own sprayer at the time?"

"Yeah, I had my own crop-dusting business for twenty-two years. Once I started into this, I saw this was better and sold all that stuff. It was too much of a struggle to keep it all."

"You do this during fire season. What do you do in January?"

"In January, I am flying a 747 for Southern Air Transport, a freighter."

I look at him hard for a moment.

"A 747," I say. "Which would you rather be doing?"

"Both. I just love to fly. It doesn't matter. When I finish with this, I'm happy to do this, and then I'm ready to do that. At the beginning of fire season, I ask for a leave of absence there. By the time that time comes around, I'm ready to get out of that freighter and do this. It works out for me."

"Do you remember your first flight on a fire?"

"The first fire," he says. "Okay, it was in Jean, Nevada, just west of Jean. It was superwindy. I had to dive the airplane straight down a cliff to get to the fire, downwind as well. It was hairy as hell. I called my wife and kids, I have teenagers at home, and I said, 'You know, guys, I don't know what I've gotten into here. I think this is worse than crop dusting.' But I saw that the work that I was doing with the airplane was effective and helping the firemen on the ground. They're usually real young guys, real athletic and tough. In Jean, Nevada, that's not far from Death Valley. It's really hot. I saw that the work that I did was helpful. After I landed, they came over and told me I did a good job. I hadn't heard anybody say, 'Hey, you did a good job.' I hadn't heard that for maybe fifteen years. In crop dusting, you're always getting complaints from people—noise or whatever. This job, people actually come up to you and want to shake your hand. They're happy to see you. They're happy about what you did. It's rewarding in that way."

"And when there's a home we couldn't save?"

"You can't battle Mother Nature. Sometimes, there's just nothing you can do. When the wind's blowing and there's a lot of fuels and it's dry, a lot of times everybody just has to run, just get back. That's just the way it is. Every now and then, you feel like, if I had done this yesterday or that this morning or done something a little different, maybe we could have saved that property."

"Is there a story you tell first, when people ask?" I ask.

"I just don't have any great flying stories."

"That's what everyone says, before they tell me a story," I say, both of us laughing.

"Okay," he says, "I'll tell you what comes to mind. It's about crop dusting. This is what I really miss about it. I flew an open-cockpit Stearman for twenty two years, in rice country a lot of times. When you turn the airplane and you see your shadow of the biplane when you're making a turn at 50 feet high, really low. The Stearman won't pull up and turn high when it's loaded, so a lot of the turns you get up over the high lines and bank around and turn back around. The rice is in water, and it's green. The way the sun is hitting it with your shadow and everything, it's just breathtaking. It's a beautiful scene. It's like that early in the morning and late in the evening. The mornings and evenings are the great memories for me because the air is nice and scenes like that. Also, flying an open-cockpit spray plane, you smell everything you fly over. If you fly over something that smells really good, it's really refreshing. You can smell greenery. Have you been in a Cub with the door open?"

"No, I haven't."

"That's the way that is. It's almost like riding a motorcycle. When you go down into a low place that's cool, there are often temperature inversions. It will be ninety degrees seventy feet in the air, and sixty on the ground at six in the morning. It will be cold going across the field. When you pull up to turn, you hit this hot air. When you hit the hot air, you feel it, and the airplane just dogs out immediately. You feel the altitude. When you dive back into the cold air, the airplane stiffens, tightens up, and comes alive, and it's cool. It feels really good."

"Are the SEATS fun planes, when it's all said and done?"

"No. The 802 and the Dromader, they're terrible flying air-planes as far as just getting in a plane and just going to fly it. They really don't fly very well. They are rigged with a little bit of an aft CG, center of gravity, to get a higher speed and higher load carrying. They have the controls heavily servoed, so it doesn't take any effort to move them. When you put the stick to the right, for example, it just stays there, or travels fur-ther, so you have to pull it back to the center. When you're trying to fly straight in turbulence, it's terrible. You can't let go at all. Even in smooth air, they won't go straight from here to the flagpole. They're not made to fly straight. They're not that maneuverable, either, because of the weight we're carry-ing. When they're empty, if you took off empty in either one of them, you'd think you were in a fighter. But they're never empty. You're never maneuvering them empty. Once you've made your drop, you're flying straight back to the airport. In a spray plane once they get light, they're great. But they're not fun airplanes to fly. The turbulence in a firefighting airplane is something that—you can't even describe it. It's really bad sometimes. They describe turbulence as severe or extreme and all that. It has different definitions of, well, if the airplane's partially out of control, part of the time. Every now and then, you get into turbulence where, if you're counting to five, the airplane is out of control a count of two out of that five. You've got the controls one way or another. It's that turbulent. You're sometimes hitting your head even. You have to wear a helmet in these planes, not for a crash, but you're hitting your head in the structure of the airplane a lot."

We both look to the horizon again, but the smoke has disap-peared in the twilight.

"The Stearman is fun to fly as a sprayer," he says. "They were early SEATS as well. Something like that is a fun airplane to me. These things aren't fun."

* * *

8:41 PM and a third truck of retardant is about to arrive, having called for directions from the bottom of the hill. Michele smiles and puts her cap back on. "I've just locked everything up!" she says. Bob Flesch points out to her, and several others, that Tanker 10 is still flying, having not come online until two o'clock, so they can fly out until pumpkin time. Tory runs through some numbers with me.

"Tanker 22 did eight loads," she says. "10 did nine. 00 did fourteen. We pumped 97,550 gallons of retardant."

This last number brings whistles and noises of surprise from everyone near. On a dry-erase board on one wall, daily and year-to-date statistics are written large. Last year, I read, for the whole year, SEATS and Heavies combined, they pumped only 80,000 gallons. For the entire fire season. Yesterday's year-to-date number was 128,487 gallons. Now plus 97,550 more.

"For the SEATS," Tory says, "407 did twelve drops, 464 did ten drops, and 472 did twelve drops."

Someone from over by the television asks why 22 did only eight drops.

"They got diverted to Rapid City to fight the Sage Fire," Tory replies.

"Will Tanker 10 get their tenth in the forty minutes left?" I ask.

"Yes."

9:23 at night. All the planes are on the ground. The sun set half an hour ago. The air is becoming still, no longer warmed by the thermals. I can still see the Alkali Creek Fire, the one near the airport, smoldering over the ridge. The Bundy Railroad and the Pine Ridge fires still send their plumes into the sky. The runway lights have turned on. A Cessna 172 takes off. Could be any evening. Could be just a scenic flight around a pretty state in the summertime. But it's been a hell of a day. There is a pink sky behind the Beartooth and Absaroka ranges tonight.

Day 2

The next morning begins hot, dry, and cloudless. And the forecast is simple. Sunny. Windy. Highs in the 90s. Perhaps a dry thunderstorm or two toward dusk. A perfect summer day for swimming in a pool or lake or river. A perfect summer day for playing outside, for picnics under some shade tree, then perhaps cooking outside, drinks shared with neighbors. A perfect summer day for fire.

Driving toward the airport this morning, I can see a wisp from the flare up over the next ridge. Someone is still there, I think, rolling the embers, making sure the thing finally goes out, hoping the wind stays calm.

What I hear, however, are the stories from yesterday. Especially the sideways stories, the background bits. I hear the deadpan of Matt Lutz telling me about a crash near Provo, Utah. "I was doing a low kind of a cowboy approach," he said. "And then the engine quit. All I had time to do was to level the wings. I thought I could make it across runway 23. Off to the west there was a highway heading north and south. Yeah, I thought I could make it. I thought I could level my wings and make it across the highway. But my left gear caught, broke off, and spun me 180 across the highway. I ended about 50 yards short of the runway facing the opposite direction."

"What did you do?" I asked.

"I figured I was okay and opened the door and jumped out."

I hear Kevin Meekin, who did not start flying until he was twenty-seven, having gotten the flying bug while logging in Alaska, tell me about his own unexpected landing. "I had to land on the highway," he said. "I was going to Jackson Hole, Wyoming, in the middle of winter. I was just north of Island Parkway, in that area. It just happened to be the right place. My engine quit. I just happened to be within gliding distance of the highway. If I had been five miles farther or ten miles back—it's the middle of winter, the snow was that deep—it would have been bad. But I see the highway there. I'm getting lined up on it. It was a nice, long stretch. I'm thinking, 'God, if there's a car there, what am I going to do?' I plan my approach and land over right next to one of the chain-off areas, thinking, if a car is coming, I could just swoosh over a little. Luckily, there wasn't. The snow was deep. I would have flipped over for sure. I landed on the highway. The gutter was full. I could see a car coming. I got down and stopped before it got there. He pulled up and rolled down the window. Looking at me, he yelled, 'You're crazy.' I didn't have a choice. I'm alive."

And I hear people ask me if I've talked with Jerry, the South African pilot of SEAT 472, yet. "He's got a story!" they say. "But you better get to him quick. The story gets better every time he tells it."

In an hour or so, I know Michele will begin the day at the tanker base with the morning weather report, and then Bob Flesch will explain the day's challenges and obligations. Tory will call out the time when the first tanker gets rolling. But first, I have a breakfast meeting with Earl Dahl, pilot of Tanker 10, the old P2 with the glass nose, the oldest plane on-site. In 2004, the government grounded thirty-three Heavy tankers, P2s and P3s, because no one knew the service life of the airplanes. The P3s were inspected, and eight of them came back to service quickly. The P2s took a little longer, but last year nine of them were given the okay and awarded contracts.

Earl looks about sixty years old, with an old-fashioned flat-top crew cut, glasses, and a bright smile. His flight suit has one sleeve nearly torn off, and he wears it with pride. When we set up the meeting, he told me about a breakfast place downtown called Stella's. "It's been in two or three places," he says. "It's moved a bit, but it's always the same people. It's really good." So at seven o'clock I tell the hostess I'm waiting for another person, and then find myself in a back booth with a cup of coffee.

Earl doesn't show. I wait. I drink more coffee. I wait. I order breakfast, and then suddenly there's Earl, holding his own breakfast, having been placed in the one booth or table I could not see when I looked around. "There I was cursing you out," he says. "And now here you are!" His smile is huge and genuine, and he sets his breakfast, a bowl of oatmeal, on the table just like he was at home. I almost feel guilty for my Godzilla-sized omelet.

Earl, it turns out, is almost my neighbor. He has a farm in Bemidji, Minnesota, not five miles from where my son is spending two weeks at the Concordia College French Language Village, just a short morning's drive from my home in Moorhead. We talk about places we both know, and then I'm not entirely sure how we get started, but as if there was nothing more natural, Earl gets to telling stories about the old days.

"I bought a Luscombe 8E," he says. "It wasn't really my first cross-country. I had my private license. It was maybe my second cross-country, or third, or whatever. Took off bright and early from Tracy, California, on the third of July. I got to Bemidji on the fourth. I stopped in Bismarck to see buddies of mine I went to high school with. The next morning I took off for Bemidji. My uncle and my grandfather lived on a farm up there. When I got up there, my grandfather was up on the roof. But he was deaf. I tried to buzz him to get his attention because I had been calling on the phone, and he doesn't hear it. So I got back in the plane—I'd landed in Bemidji to get fuel. Went out there. Buzzed the house. Never saw me. Nothing. But anyway, the next couple of days I asked my uncle and him if he wanted to go for an airplane ride. My uncle wanted nothing to do with it. But Grandpa, he was up for anything. You know, he had to use a cane to walk. And a Luscombe wasn't an easy plane to get in and out of."

"You started flying when you were seventeen? Eighteen?" I ask.

"Oh, no, no, no. I started late. I moved up to California, always interested in airplanes. But I never quite . . . Nobody ever said, 'Well, let's go out to the airport. You give me money, and I'll teach you how to fly.' Then this guy, who became a good friend of mine, his name was John Caruso, he was a maintenance guy. We got to talking, and pretty soon we realized that we both liked airplanes, and he was taking flying lessons. He asked me. He said, 'Do you want to go with me one of these days? I have to rent a bigger airplane because it's got a radio in it.'"

"What were you taking lessons in then?"

"A Cessna 150. Then John, who was taking flying lessons before I did, bought a Luscombe from his flight instructor. The very Luscombe I ended up buzzing Grandpa with. So he kept on getting his ratings; pretty soon he had a flight-instructor rating. He said, 'Buy the airplane from me. I'll give you all the flight instructions free.' He said, 'You've to build time anyway.' I said, 'Okay.' So I did. And he did. I flew that thing all over. In fact, when he got his commercial pilot's license rating, we went up to a town called Susanville, California. There was a lady up there by the name of Mary Barr. She was the first woman pilot in the country for the Forest Service. She eventually became—I think she retired as the head of aviation for the Forest Service. This was many years later. I ended up going up there and getting my commercial pilot's license from her. I remember one day we were up there flying around at Mount Lassen. It was the middle of winter. I hitchhiked up there. No, that was later. I flew my airplane up there. We were flying one of her airplanes because I had to do something and didn't have that in that little Luscombe, and we're flying over Mount Lassen, and this guy who was taking lessons up there from Mrs. Barr also went along. We were looking down, and there's all kinds of snow down there. The wind was blowing. It looks like North Dakota in the wintertime except it's a little more peaked. And he says, 'Boy, how would you like be down with just a pair of spurs and a necktie on?' I've never forgotten that. That's what I think about when I take a coat!"

One of Stella's waitresses comes over and asks if I'd like some Tabasco sauce for my omelet, which causes both Earl and me to laugh out loud.

"Anyway," he says, "I got my commercial license from her. Then I bounced around and did all kinds of flying. I flew for Zantop Air Transport, the old Zantop out of Detroit. Ferried airplanes. That was my first flying job where I actually got paid. Ferried them all over the country, down into Guatemala. Crop dusters mostly, but some Piper stuff. A lot of Piper products. Mostly Piper Pawnees."

"How'd you wind up flying Tanker 10?" I ask.

"Lynch Flying Service, which used to be based here in Billings. You've been down to tanker base. Have you seen those two B-26 Invaders sitting there? Red, white, and blue one? And behind that there's what they call a K model. It's green. It's olive green. It's sitting right there. The red, white, and blue one is from the movie *Always*. That was Denny Lynch. In '76, I was flying fire patrol. In '76, they had a big fire season in Minnesota. That's what I was doing, flying fire patrol for the fires in Minnesota, Chippewa National Forest, Bemidji State Forest, and Red Lake Indian Reservation. Get one or the other during the day. I'd kinda gotten away from aviation a little bit. And we flew every day."

"What were you flying?"

"152! Well, Denny Lynch had the B-26. He used to have about five or six at that time. He actually was in Hibbing, Minnesota. One day, they had a fire up in Red Lake. These B-26s started coming in to get retardant. I walked up there and asked the first guy, 'Hey, are you Denny Lynch?' He says, 'No, but he's right behind me.' Okay. Sure enough. A little bit later a B-26. 'Are you Denny Lynch?' Those airplanes you had to get up on the top of the fuselage to watch them load the plane. He said, 'Nope, but he's right behind me.' This went on until finally the fourth airplane came in, and it was Denny Lynch. 'Hey,' I said, 'I understand you're looking for some pilots.' He said, 'Do you know anything about this airplane?' 'No,' I said, 'but I used to fly a c-36, which has the very same engine as the B-26.' He says, 'You did?' I said, 'Yeah. For Zantop Air Transport.' 'Oh, wow. How would you like to go for a ride and see what this is all about?' 'Yeah!' 'Come over to Hibbing, and I'll give you a ride.' I said I'd be over tomorrow, which I did. When I got there, he was just taxiing out, but he saw me by the fence. Turned around. Parked. I ran out there. Got in the plane—of course, you can't do that nowadays. Jumped in the plane; off we went. I think it was two or three days later we got back there. We went to northern Minnesota, and then back down to Brainerd to get a load. There was a fire by the Anoka County Airport. Went down there. Did a drop. It was at night. We got in a little trouble. We spent the night in Minneapolis at the Thunderbird Hotel by the airport. Went back up the next day. It was November. It was just superdry in Minnesota in '76. Finally, some day there in November, it finally snowed a little bit, just barely. We hardly ever had any snow at all that year. That was the end of the fire season. Denny said, 'Well, if you're interested, come on out to Billings.' I did next year and went flying with one of their other pilots. Then the next year, '78, he turned me loose in one of his B-26s."

"When did Tanker 10 come along?" I ask.

"Oh, God. This year. I flew Neptunes, but I flew for Hawkins and Powers for fourteen years. I flew for Evergreen, and I flew for Arnold Kolb, which was Black Hills Aviation. That's the company that Mr. Timmons bought and turned into Neptune."

"Tell me about flying yesterday?"

"Yesterday was fun! We were just doing all kinds of structure protection. Myself and the others were putting lines down, boxes around things. That one kid who was sitting out there at the picnic table flying Air Attack? He's one of the smoke jumpers that I used to fly years ago out of Silver City. We were yakking out there about how this fire, we dropped on the north side of this place. Half of our load was left, so we dropped a line in front of this place. Came back here, reloaded. By the time we got back, that fire had just roared right up to the house. You could just barely see the house in the smoke. We didn't hardly recognize everything like that at first because it had changed: smoke, fire, burnt. We finally thought, 'Oh, that's the place we dropped next to, on the north side.' It was so desperate by that time. The Air Attack says, 'Just drop on the house.' So we came around, dropped half a load just to the north side of the house. Came back around and did it again. Maybe we'll find out today if it made it."

"Is Tanker 10 that nimble?"

"There's one copilot I used to have. When we'd check into a motel, we'd say, 'Have you got a commercial rate?' Sometimes they'd say, 'No, but we've got a truckers' rate.' I'd say, 'Hey, great. We're driving a truck.' Somebody would say, 'What kind?' We'd say, 'A belly dumper!' It's a good airplane. It's heavy. Not super-maneuverable. It's got a lot of power. It is fun to fly. It's not hard to handle, but it's heavy. No question about that."

"What's it like when you dump the load?"

"Not a whole lot changes if you're not going too fast."

"You're at 200 feet? Something like that?"

"I think the Forest Service wants you at 175." Earl looks around, as if someone is listening, and laughs. "I shouldn't say it that way—'I think.'"

"How fast are you going?"

"I try to fly 130 knots. At that speed, you still have nice control. Not too fast—I mean, you're not just screaming. That airplane gets notorious for, once you put the nose over, it just wants to go like crazy. Neptune has installed spoilers. This airplane had spoilers, but it was strictly for control, turning left to right. The spoiler on the side that you wanted to turn would come up, the other one would stay down. But then they rigged up a deal on it. You push a button on the throttle, and both spoilers come up. It really improves your chances of pushing the nose down and maintaining that speed. This summer we were down in Sedona—that was on the news. We were dropping there. That was pretty spectacular, first for the view of Sedona, the red rock and all that. We were coming through a notch by Highway 89/80 there and then down. We were really going down. If you'd get the plane set up, you could maintain 130 knots going down. That's pretty neat. Otherwise, you're just screaming down through there. We try not to do that. In fact, we don't do that. There's some limits."

The waitress clears our plates and pours more coffee, and Earl tells me about flying Twin Otters for three years in Chad, working for a company that had a contract with Esso Oil. When the bill comes and we begin to walk to the door, I have one more question.

"I'm going to ask a really ignorant question here," I say. "I should know this, but I don't. When you're targeting a drop, have you got anything like a bombsight in that plane, or is it just experience?"

"Kentucky windage," he says, laughing. "I was talking with Bill Waltman, another pilot. We were exchanging stories one day. I was telling about in Salt Lake City one year a long time ago. I was flying for Evergreen. There was a fire on Wasatch Mountains, way up on top. It wasn't doing much. Clear day, kind of cool for the summer. A lot of wind coming off the lake, coming from that direction anyway, hitting the Wasatches and then going up. I came along, and the guy said (there was just one guy up there)—it was grass and some light brush burning—he says, 'Could you hit this?' I said, 'Yeah.' I came along on the right. It was right at the very top. I came down the ridge, dropped that retardant. It just took off with the wind to the next county."

"Oh, Lord," I say. "Every sprayer's nightmare."

"I said, 'Let me try something.' I went around. This time I came back, and the fire is up here," Earl puts one hand over his head. "And I'm down here." Earl holds his other hand down by his knees. "I punched it off. The wind just took that retardant right up the smoke and dropped it right on it. The guy says, 'That was perfect. Can you do that again?' I said, 'Yeah, I can do it ten more times.' It just carried it right up. I don't know far down I was. The first time I did it was just a guess."

"In 10, have you got just a trigger, or have you got one of those computers?"

"We have a little computer of sorts, not as fancy as the AeroUnion ones have. You just set it up for coverage level. The Lead planes or the Air Attack will ask you for a coverage level. A lot of times out here we'll use four because the fuel is light enough. We'll eventually get into something, timber or something like that, and you set up using heavier coverage levels. Out here yesterday, I think one time somebody else asked for three, and somebody even asked for a two. Again, Kentucky windage and a little bit of experience. Like on that house that we dropped on. The wind was blowing. The house was here, so we had to find a drop over here, and up high enough. It would just kind of rain down on it. Again, we'll find out today if it's still there. I did that once before in Colorado. In 1994 they had a heck of a fire season. That was the year of the Storm King Mountain tragedy. All those jumpers and firefighters died. That was on Storm King Mountain. Anyway, before that happened, Payonia, Colorado, there was this fire. It was just going up the hill like this. There was a house there. The Lead plane pilot, who I know real well, used to be a smoke jumper. A lot of Lead plane pilots used to be smoke jumpers. I said, 'Hey do I need to come around and go underneath the column?' It was going like this. Here's the spot where the house was. The smoke column was going right up over it. Plenty of visibility. He said, 'I've been in it many times. It's no big deal.' So, okay, we went around. We came in line. He says, 'See the house?' I go, 'Yup.' He says, 'Just hit in front of it. You know, between it and the fire.' I did. Go around and do it again. I put the other half—a wider swath. Turned around. Did it again. Left. When we got back—we were out there again—the fire had moved. I said, 'How's that house doing?' He says, 'I don't know. I haven't looked.' Several days later, I had a day off. I had it in my head I was going to drive up there and see how that house did. I drove up there. Sure enough, the house was still there. The only thing that had happened, it had a big, old glass sliding door, first floor, that faced where the fire was coming up. It cracked it. I don't know if it was cracked before the fire. Then it had a little deck. One of the posts of the deck had singed. That was it. Then, there was a farmer, rancher, whatever next door. I saw him. I drove over there because one of the loads before that, he was trying to build his own fire line with his tractor with some farm implement. I walked over and told him who I was. He says, 'Oh, yeah, are you the guy who dropped them?' I said, 'Yeah.' He was building a fire line, and we came right and built a fire line for him. He said, 'Hey, yeah. Thanks a lot.' I said, 'You're welcome.'"

* * *

8:00 AM at the tanker base. Another truck full of retardant has shown up and sits idling by the tanks. Everyone is here, waiting on the porch, talking on cell phones in the parking lot. The sun is bright, and the air has moved from warm already to hot. But there's a temperature inversion out at the fires. All the smoke is being held to the ground, and there's no way to see where to drop. The firefighters on the ground are having a hell of a time. But until the inversion lifts, there's no one calling for a tanker.

Bill gives me a tour of Tanker 10. Climbing up on a ladder in the nose wheel well, it takes some twists and turns to get into the pilot's seat, and then I crash my head into a lever as I'm trying to get out. In the back of the plane, there's a surfboard hung from one of the walls.

On the ramp, Jim walks one way, Michele walks another.

They check radios, Pit 1 and 2 hoses, the switches and valves by the tanks. Allen goes by, raises his eyebrows to me, and smiles. "Soon enough!" he says. In the tanker base, Tory organizes the cards and papers in front of her. "Rolling!" I say. "At least someone is," she replies. "If I had a card for you, I'd punch it in."

In truth, everyone is waiting. So when Jerry walks by, we meet and grab a spot at one of the tables on the deck.

"Everybody calls me Jerry," he says. "My name is actually Gert. My last name is Marais."

"You're from South Africa," I say.

"Well, I actually live in Fort Benton, Montana, for the last six years. We moved over here six years ago due to the political situation back in South Africa. I was a firefighting pilot over there. When I came over here, they were in need of a SEAT pilot, so I jumped in. Ever since then, I am still here."

Jerry's voice has the accent of the former British colony, soft in the morning shade.

"My dad was a rancher," he says, "in a little town called Ficksburg. It's right in the eastern, southeastern part of the country in a province called the Eastern Free State. Our neighbor was a crop duster. I used to go out and mix chemical for him when I was a little kid, during holidays and things like that. Part of my pay was to get a ride back with him at nighttime. That just caught my interest. After my military career—I was an infantry soldier—I started getting into the flying. That's been about twenty years now that I've been in the flying. I flew before I started firefighting and crop dusting. I flew for various outfits, you know, including the UN and the Red Cross in Africa, doing several missions. I was flying King Air 200s and Caravans. Those types of airplanes. Then, I had an opportunity back in the '90s to buy a Dromader to spray with, but it came with a fire contract. I thought, 'Well, let's go and try to do firefighting.' That's how I ended up in firefighting. Since then, I just loved it so much that I just stayed in the fire business."

"Is it just the thrill and the rush? Is that what attracted you to it?"

"Yeah, I guess. Apart from the—I always liked the crop dusting. The firefighting was just much more of a thrill, especially when like here, like yesterday was an example. When you get out here and you have to save a house, you got to save livestock and stuff like that, and the things are working out, I like that."

I tell him his friends have been warning me there's a story from yesterday.

"Oh, yeah. It was the day before yesterday. We were out on a fire, the Railroad Fire. The Lead plane would normally guide us right in there. Then he clears the line for us with the Air Attack, who radios the ground crew and gets them out of the line. Apparently, there was no communication. The guys didn't want to clear the line. Several flights we made back and forth to get the guys out of the line."

"Do you want my two cents' worth on this?" Jim Hassler has come into the building. "I don't believe a word he says." Everyone laughs.

"Didn't they know what you were trying to do?"

"No, they didn't know what I was trying to do. At that point in time, they didn't know what to expect. Sometimes you have private guys out there. It might be private land too where there's private guys. They don't know how the system works. Whenever there's a fire on private land and it heads toward BLM or Forest Service land, you know the BLM and Forest Service guys would jump right in there and help the firefighters to put it out. The deal was so yesterday or the day before what happened was, when we got in there, they didn't clear the line at that point in time because of the radio communication. I told the Lead guy that I have a PA system on board with a speaker and a siren. He was kind of surprised. I said, okay, well, I'll clear the line for him. He let me in there. As I came in, I got on the speaker and hit the siren. I said to the guys, 'This is the sheriff. Clear the line immediately.' So everybody just scattered and rushed to get out of the way."

"Did you see them running away?"

"Yeah, it worked pretty good. One guy had an engine on the ground. An engine is one of these pickups that sprays. He thought it wasn't funny, so he kind of showed me a little sign with his hand."

"Yesterday," I say, "everyone seemed to think it was a losing battle. Even you came in and said the fire was rolling right over every line the tankers put down."

"No, I don't think really yesterday was unsuccessful. I think every drop really counts. I remember on my last load, I was doing a protection around the tower, some structure protection. As I came in to do my drop, I hit a bump so hard that my fingers slipped off the button. And so it closed my gate up, so I had to do the exercise over again. That happens. In general, yesterday I think was really a very good day. I feel really good about the houses that were saved and the cattle and everything that were saved. Because in the past, I've seen houses burn down. I've seen livestock burn and died. It's bad. Yesterday, I think we did really good. But there is a problem," he goes on. "I'm turning forty-one years old this year. I'm probably one of, I think I can count on my one hand, I think I'm probably one of the youngest guys in this industry. Matt, that's flying with me, is the only kid that I know that's younger than me, and probably another kid down South. There is not many guys around that does this job."

"Is there a next generation coming up, or is this going to be a problem in ten years?"

"That's what I'm saying. I'm forty-one years old, you know, and I am one of the younger guys in this industry. If you look at the heavier tanker guys, it's all guys in their sixties and late fifties. And even in our industry, everybody is in their high forties into sixties."

"There are a lot of sprayers out there, though," I say.

"There are a lot of sprayers. There's a difference between sprayers and firefighting guys. Firefighting is like the military. Everything is basically done the same, the organization. Firefighting pilots need to go through a school to understand it. Many firefighting guys get there and say, 'No, this is not for me. I don't like to talk on the radio,' or 'No, that's not how we do it,' or 'No, I don't want to do that.' They don't want to get into the discipline flying-type deal where you have to be at a specific altitude. You've got to report every fifteen minutes. They don't like it. They just have that crop-dusting image. That's how they want to stay. That's why some guys are also too afraid. I talked to many crop-duster pilots before who said, no, they will never do the job that we do. The difference is they fly when it's nice, quiet mornings, wind doesn't blow. When the wind blows, they stand down. This is the opposite with us. We fly when it's rough, the wind is going bad, in mountainous terrain. Most crop dusters never flew in mountains. That's why they have a fear for that. Back in 2004, we lost three of our pilots in three months. It was a pretty sad deal for me. It was all three friends of mine. It kind of puts you back a little bit. You know, it always reminds you to check certain things better. It's all pilot error. Two of those pilots flew into the ground, misjudging themselves. One guy flew into bad weather and just couldn't get out and flew into the mountain. That's one thing—we have a policy now with the company. It comes back to the crop-duster image. People get to feel like when the wind blows, 'I'll go. I'll show these guys. I'll do it.' It doesn't work like that. I am the chief pilot of the company. What I'm doing is, when it goes to about thirty-mile-an-hour winds and gets really rough, one guy out there reports it's really rough, then we make everybody stand down. We don't have this one guy feel like 'I'm left behind, and this guy thinks he's hot.' We make everybody stand down. Everybody's on the same page. We make it safe. We get back. When the conditions are good, we fly again."

* * *

Finally, the morning briefing begins with Michele giving the weather report. Temperatures into the hundreds today, no rain expected. Another hot, windy, and dry day. Bob takes over then, and again the conversation is all about radio frequencies. Yesterday, there was too much conversation on too few frequencies, and people were often confused or distracted. There's a long discussion about what frequencies people are going to use, whom they should be talking to, and although the procedure they've set up, which actually works, is a little outside of FAA regulations, everyone is comfortable with it. Bob reports that a good amount of extra equipment is coming in today. More SEATS. More Heavy tankers.

Michele makes a point at the end. With so much traffic on the ramp, Jim won't be able to handle it all by himself, so she's going to be up there helping. Yesterday, apparently, one of the Heavy tanker pilots complained about "trainees" working in the pits. After the meeting, two or three people walk by Michele and say, "Nicely done."

The dance begins again.

11:05 in the morning and 535 Sierra Alpha, the Air Attack plane, taxis away from the tanker base. It is the first plane out this morning, and the pilot is Randy Lynch, the grandson of Denny Lynch, who hired Earl. "I'm the only one who has it in my blood," he tells me, speaking about his siblings.

11:24. Michele walks out and says, "We're going!" The pilots head to their planes.

11:31. The engines on the Lead plane, the Beech 90, are fired up. The pilots are in all three SEATS waiting for dispatch sheets. On the porch, the conversation continues about combining the TFRS for the Pine Ridge and Bundy Railroad fires into one.

11:33. Joe cranks the turbine in 407, and the plane shudders to life. Tory sends the assignment sheets from the office out to the cockpits.

11:34. Matt starts SEAT 464.

11:35. Jerry starts SEAT 472.

Pulling up to the pit, it's Matt and then Joe and then Jerry in a line.

11:37 and 776 Delta Charlie, the Lead plane, rolls away from the ramp.

11:38. SEAT 464 is done loading and pulls away from Pit 1. SEAT 407 pulls up to take its place and load. At Pit 2, Jim and Earl pull the tubes to pump the retardant over to the plane and connect them to the belly. The Lead plane rolls down the runway.

11:41. Joe in 407 rolls away from Pit 1. Jerry in 472 rolls in behind him. Matt takes off. Jerry dumps the water ballast pumped into his tank last night onto Pit 1. The crew connects the hoses to pump fresh retardant in.

11:43. SEAT 407 begins it takeoff roll.

11:45. Jerry pulls away from the pit.

11:47. Jim disconnects the hose from Tanker 10. SEAT 472 begins its takeoff roll.

11:50. Tanker 10 fires up its first engine. Jim tries to reach people on the ramp radio, but his transmission is all broken and garbled. When the old piston engine catches, a thick plume of white oil smoke coughs out the back. This is the way an airplane engine should start, I think. A sight from the old days. The second engine begins immediately afterward. Jim yells, "When this one's done, we're going to run the system." Then he takes off his headset, and tosses it with his radio into the grass. "These radios don't work worth shit!"

11:54. The wheels begin rolling, and Tanker 10 pulls away from Pit 2. Tanker 22 pulls up for its turn. Tanker 00 is off today. Tanker 27, another P3, should be here sometime in the afternoon.

Noon. Tanker 10 begins to roll down the runway.

12:08. With only three engines running, the fourth just beginning to spin, Tanker 22 pulls away from Pit 2 and heads toward the runway.

12:10. Tanker 22 is in the sky.

12:15. SEAT 407 is already back from its first run, then 464, then 472. "In the blocks," Tory calls over the radio, stamping the cards into the clock. And then a few minutes later, "Rolling." On the radio, I can hear the instructions again. Load and return.

I walk outside and around the building and look to the east again. The sun has risen a bit in the sky. The angles of light have changed. What I see all across the northern and eastern horizons is a fat, low band of gray smoke blanketing the horizon, and then the silhouette of Tanker 10 on its way back to base. Load and return.

* * *

Tanker 27 has a serious problem. It arrived an hour ago, got fuel and retardant, and then one of its engines went bad. The starter brake won't release. This isn't a problem you fix on-site, I'm told. This is the kind of problem where you fly the plane back home on three engines, then drop the bad one and take it apart. But the problem now is that it's got a full load of retardant. They can't take off on three engines with a full load. Bob Flesch and Allen meet at Pit 1 to talk about options.

SEAT 472 is parked on the ramp. Something's gone wrong with the engine's cooling, Jerry says. The cowling is open, and a mechanic peers inside.

The pilots of Tanker 27 want to get out of town. Someone suggests they simply dump their load over at Edwards and wash it into the sewer. Someone else suggests they off-load it into a holding tank of some sort.

One of the new SEATs has shown up, SEAT 423, but it too rests parked on the ramp. The pilot is eating. Then there's a briefing, the list of radio frequencies, the dispatch sheets.

3:35 in the afternoon. Allen decides that Tanker 27 is going to sit over at Edwards Jet Center until things calm down. Then they'll taxi it over and off-load it into the 5,000-gallon tank for premixed mud. Then Jim has the idea that they can pump off 27's slurry into a truck and take it out to Roundup, a small town here where they stage mud for SEATS that need to land there. At one point, Tory looks up and says, "This is worse than yesterday. You've got a tanker that's broken down. You've got a SEAT that's broken down. You have the new SEATS showing up. Dispatch, apparently, changes where planes are going every five minutes, then they call over here to ask where planes are going. They're the ones who make the decisions."

Listening to dispatch, I hear Air Attack over the Bundy Railroad Fire ask for Tanker 10 to come back. The fire is about a mile from a ranch house. As they are calling in, Tanker 10 pulls up to Pit 2 for reloading.

Another new SEAT, 475, arrives at 4:30.

* * *

Bob Flesch is a quiet person, but also clearly the person involved with a larger picture. You can tell when he's in the room, because suddenly everyone's eyes are tracking in the same direction. His title is unit aviation manager. In the tanker base, that means he's the boss. But his style is cooperative.

"So what's all this look like from your chair?" I ask him.

"You know," he says, "I really don't know. I've only been here four weeks. I don't have anything to compare it to."

Before here, he tells me, he was a crew coordinator for a Bureau of Indian Affairs Type 2 crew. Before that, he was with helitack, smoke jumping.

"How did you wind up doing this?" I ask. "It opened; you were interested?"

"Yeah. I had a little bit of a fixed-wing background. I primarily came up in the rotor aspect of the fire and worked with the fixed-wing and SEAT operations and such. The position came out, so I applied. They must have been desperate."

"So this is the average day now, eh?"

"Yeah, I assume, every ten minutes, something new comes up. You just have to roll with the punches and reset priorities constantly. It's a pleasant change. Hopefully, it's working out. I guess it's like anything. You come into a new position—a lot of stuff I didn't know what to expect. There's been plenty of surprises."

"Like what?"

"I guess just the overall complexity of all the things that I have to do in this position, or attempt to do in this position."

Bob grins at me, at the small bit of self-effacing.

"Like this morning," he goes on. "I come in before seven to unload two trucks of retardant. I have to try to get ready for a briefing, as much as we can. As you can see, it's quite a dynamic operation, and stuff changes so fast. So we have a briefing, and then we start flying immediately. Then we go into the realm of trying to set priorities for where the Heavy air tankers will go and where the SEATs are going. Additional aircraft flying in. Air Attack gets a call and tells dispatch. Then, when dispatch gets that, they're also getting calls from neighboring agencies as well as Northern Rockies, which is the coordination center here in Montana, for heavier aircraft to go different places. I am, immediately, trying to juggle where the Heavy aircraft are going. Right now, I think, Tanker 10 is headed down to Wyoming because there's a community threatened."

"Is it your call, finally, where to go?"

"Yeah. It has been. I guess I wasn't expecting that. It seems like a lot of responsibility. We just try to do the best that we could do with the information that we have. I'm sure it doesn't make everybody happy, but with limited resources we can only do what we can."

"After the briefing, does your day become mostly reactive?"

"Yeah, it becomes very reactive. You can do all the finding what you want to try to be proactive. But then 27 lands and breaks down immediately. What are you going to do? We're thinking we're going to have three Heavies fly in today. Of course, we're down to two again. Now, if Tanker 10 is gone, we'll be down to one."

"What does your wife think of all this?"

"She knows it's part of it. It's kinda funny. One of the reasons I got out of the helicopter world of fires was so I could be home more."

"Are you home more?"

"No."

"At least not this week?"

"Exactly. It was pretty tough the other day. My little one is three and a half. I was talking to him on the phone. He goes, 'Can you come over?' So that was pretty hard."

Phones ring in the background, and people appear at the door. Michele comes in and says they need a timekeeper like Tory over in Miles City, and asks if she can go. "No," Bob says simply. Someone else comes in and tells Bob that one of the new SEAT pilots is only a level-two pilot and needed to have the air-space chart explained to him. Bob takes it in and nods. A third person comes in wanting to know the severity request, which is an official request for the resources that get allocated here. Bob's answer is "The works."

* * *

6:20 in the evening. Tory is nearly frantic because somebody who was supposed to pick up her kids hasn't. The kids are waiting. She has to leave.

Earl comes in the building and grabs a plastic bag filled with two boxed suppers for himself and his copilot, a man named Bill Ethridge and nicknamed William the Large because he's very tall and stocky. "A big boy!" Earl says. And it's clear that Earl is having a tremendous day. "Just like being at Boy Scouts camp!" he says, looking at his supper. Big smile on his face. Then he's out right away and back in Tanker 10, ready to fly.

Tory talks with Bob and goes over a list of people she can call to take her place, and finally she calls a woman named Angel, a former timekeeper, who comes in and replaces her. On the ramp radio, a pilot reports, "Angel! It's good to hear your voice again!"

Tanker 22 is going to Wyoming. The pilots and mechanics grab flight bags and duffel bags and all pile in. They're packed for several days, always are, and no one knows where they'll go or how long they'll be gone. Greg Hock, the pilot of Tanker 22, stands by the door of the tanker base. "It's a mess from here to Rapid City." The active fires here are Bundy Railroad, Pine Ridge, and then two smaller ones, Sage and Thorn Divide. Thorn Divide is in Wyoming.

7:15 in the evening. Lewistown, northwest of Billings, is calling in a new fire, a new start. When Bob's cell phone rings with the news, he leans back, grimaces, puts a hand to his stomach like he is being impaled with a sword. They need what's called Initial Attack, most likely a SEAT. Start-ups get priority. Bob has a meeting in his office with Mark Verlanic, a more seasoned base manager who has been quietly working every corner of the operation, to coordinate the resources and the allocation of the airplanes.

Coming up at 9 o'clock at night, it's not quite pumpkin time yet, but it's too dark or too close to it to send out another load. The SEATS are all in, being parked over at Edwards. Tanker 27 is pulled over to Pit 1, where they're going to try to off-load the belly full of slurry until it's light enough to fly, and then the three-engine ferry flight home where the fourth engine will simply be replaced. Bob is working on ordering a Type 1 Air Attack aircraft. Multiengine. Multiradio. He's got an open order for one. For a day or so, they haven't been able to find a plane, but finally they found one. The pumps start running, and Tanker 27 is beginning its off-load into the tanks.

Families, wives and young children, friends, and neighbors show up on the deck again, to watch the planes come in. After 9:00 p.m., Bob is still here. Allen is still here. Angel is still here, at the radio. Helicopters fly low over the tanker base and land at Edwards. It's a tough place to walk away from. There's always something urgent, something necessary that has to be done. Even the waiting is waiting around for that thing, whatever it may be, that is going to arrive next and need immediate attention now.

As I head toward the Jeep, I'm met in the parking lot by a lone mule deer, which I swear looks lost and confused. And when I get to the hotel, the TV beeps. Civil authorities have issued a civil-emergency message for Yellowstone County effective until midnight. Residents in Custer should prepare for possible evacuation. Residents four miles east of Waco are ordered to evacuate immediately.

Day 3

As I walk up to the tanker base, I see one, two, three, four, five tankers of retardant lined up to off-load into the tanks. The day's dawning is bright and clear. I can see hills and rises that weren't visible yesterday or the day before. Yet off in the distance, still those terrible plumes of smoke. When I see Bob, I ask him what time he left last night. He tells me he didn't, but he did lay down about two o'clock for a bit.

Three minutes before 9:00, and Tanker 27 takes off with three engines, the props on the fourth fully feathered, and starts his way back to Chico, California.

Everyone gathered again on the tanker-base deck, Bob begins the briefing with a discussion of TFRs. Pine Ridge has been expanded. He hopes to have Bundy Railroad expanded by noon. Michele does a run-through of the weather. There's a fire weather watch, she says, and a few people fake surprise. Temperature one hundred degrees, she says. Humidity in single digits. Bob says the Northern Rockies office and the national office were upset that a plane wasn't send to Wyoming right away yesterday. Bob tells the pilots to make sure they call back and say whether a structure is a residence or not. They're setting priorities. Bob asks how the radio procedures worked yesterday, given all the confusion the day before. Still too much going on, he learns.

"One thing," he says just before the meeting is over. "Unless you hear differently, all planes are load and return. Load and return until further notice."

There are already requests for tankers. Air Attack has been gone for twenty minutes. Someone teases Earl about the torn sleeve on his flight suit, and he simply laughs. Jim and Michele head out to the pits, and the pilots are fast behind them. Once again, the turbines and pistons fire up, and the tanker base moves into high gear.

Tory is back on the radio. Patient and comforting. It is, I think, amazing work. Necessary work. But as soon as I think this, I know I am wrong. In the back of my head, I can hear Angel, yesterday, greeting every pilot and loader who came through the door.

"Strong work, guys," Angel said. "Strong work."

Epilogue

★ ★ ★ ★

At twilight, the ramp is often a beautiful place.

On the other side of the airport here at Hector Field, scheduled airlines come and go, and passengers leave the airplanes through jetways into terminals, without once stepping outside into weather or birdsong. Their baggage is brought to them, and they rush to cars and family and home, or perhaps just to hotels and then meetings in the morning. There is talk about flight delays and turbulence, or airplane food, but anything real about the flying remains invisible. They may have been watching out the window as the jet flared and set its tires to the runway, but looking sideways out a window tells you nothing about the feel of the thing in the air. And that small window misses everything. In the old days, passengers boarded and disembarked via stairways rolled to an airplane's side, and there was that time and space between the terminal and the aircraft. There was that time and space to taste the transition.

Walking out to the 152 this evening, I meet Brandon, one of the flight instructors, on his way in. A young woman named Amy is with him, a huge smile on her face that does not weaken while we chat.

"Heading out?" he asks me.

"Night cross-country," I tell him. "Just up to Grand Forks and back."

Brandon smiles, and tells me he and his student had just

been up on a practice cross-country flight, checking out some waypoints, and it's clear she had a good time. It's clear she cannot find the words to express how the world has changed.

"Have fun!" Brandon says, and as I turn toward the 152 I assure him I will.

The preflight is easy, and although it's fast for me now, it's also particular and detailed. My hand runs the length of each blade of the propeller, and I remember, every time, that first flight that did not happen. When everything is ready, I have a moment to linger and watch.

The sun sets below the horizon, and the lights of the airport grow brighter. Blue lights for the taxiways. White lights for the runways. The black and white and red of the intersection markers. The flashing yellow lights at the run-up areas just before the runways. The air grows still as the stars come out, and in the sky I can see the strobes and beacons and landing lights of airplanes coming home. Standing on the north ramp, one hand on an airplane I am about to fly, watching the sky and what it holds transform, I would be lying if I said it was anything less than filled with magic and beauty.

For pilots, *night* is an official term. It begins half an hour after sunset, what the tanker pilots call pumpkin time, and ends half an hour before sunrise. And because I need to log some official night flying, I have to wait a few minutes before Mark joins me and we see how well I can navigate and fly at night. So I simply look at the planes parked near me. There is a Cirrus, and a Piper Warrior. There is a Cessna 182, and two Cessna 172s. There are six Cessna 340s, flown by the extraordinary pilots of a company called Weather Modification, Inc., who fly into the heart of thunderstorms to seed the clouds and divert or lessen the rain and the hail. And, of course, there is the little red and white 152.

This moment, I suddenly understand, is one of the important ones, one of the connecting ones. The ramp, I understand, is simply one of those places of huge and tremendous potential. When I walk out here, I am doing what every other pilot has always done. Even though I am here at the beginning of a soft late-summer night on the northern prairie, I am walking with Steve on his way to a Twin Otter in Resolute, and Earl on his way to Tanker 10, with Dallas on his way to a WC-130, and with Tim on his way to the Bell 222. Every one of us walks to a craft that will put us in the air, that will put our talents and energies into the wind. On the ramp, we are all before the story about to be lived, and that potential is one way to be fully awake and fully alive.

Mark comes out, and soon enough we have the small plane heading north in the nighttime sky. Finding Grand Forks is easy, as is landing on runway 35 Left. On the way back, passing the town of Hillsboro, I key the radio talk button seven times to light up the runway at the small-town airport, just to check my navigation, but even more so just because it's pretty. New stars erupt in the sky as planes turn on their landing lights, and the world itself seems to be made of lights. Car lights on highways. Barn lights at farmsteads. The blinking lights of the other airplanes—I am amazed by how many there are!—and then the cold lights from outer space that reach all the way back to the start of time. Everything, the universe, above and below us as we fly.

"Pretty, isn't it?" Mark asks me.

*   *   *

The ramp is the place of departure and potential, the place where every story turns to line 1, page 1, and the ramp is also that place of ending, of homecoming, the place where the story is closed and the pilot rests. At one level, it is the sight every pilot trusts he will see again as he pulls back on the stick or yoke and urges his aircraft into the sky. It is the place where the simple fact of your being there means job well done.

Sometimes, though, the story you have to tell is a little bit hairier, a little bit more exciting than you wish, even though you cannot wait to tell it.

Late September, a beautiful autumn day when the trees are rich and television reporters are saying now is peak color, the 152 and I are off to fill another requirement. The long solo cross-country. Last night, I filled out my flight plan, calculated the distance between waypoints, and this morning I checked the winds aloft and with my E6B wheel I figured out the wind-correction angles and ground speed and fuel burn and time to each point. Fargo to Thief River Falls. Thief River Falls to Bemidji. Bemidji back to Fargo. This was, I thought, an easy day. This was, I thought, the first day of my real flying, a day when I would simply take to the air and enjoy every river, every railway, every silver lake in the sunshine.

The airport at Thief River Falls does not have a control tower, so pilots here, like pilots at every uncontrolled airport, tune in the airport frequency on their radios and self-announce their positions and intentions. When I arrive, on time, with my plan and waypoints, I announce my position in the pattern, entering the downwind leg for right traffic, and another pilot comes on to tell me he's several thousand feet above me, turning circles to lose altitude and then land here too.

"You want to go first?" he asks me.

"I'm not in any hurry," I say. "It's all yours."

I head west, away from the airport, with no real destination other than the pleasure of looking around, and for a few minutes, until I hear that other pilot's voice tell me he's clear of the runway, the 152 and I meander in the summer sky.

The landing is easy, as is the next leg, to Bemidji, though there is a good bit more traffic. Lower Red Lake off the plane's left wing, a tank farm off the right, a sectional map on a clipboard on my lap, this is low and slow flying at its very best, I think. The landing is simple and fun. And there is a part of me that wants to park the plane and go inside someplace to find a hamburger, not because I am hungry but because I want to keep the last leg in front of me. But I also know someone else has reserved the plane for this afternoon and I need to get back.

In the air, I set my heading and wait for my first waypoint, and suddenly the left wing of the airplane rises sharply as I catch some gust of wind. It's easy to correct, but a few minutes later it happens again. My first waypoint comes too fast, and on the wrong side of the airplane. The winds have come up. The winds have come up hard.

Finding Fargo is not difficult, but what the tower tells me is not what I want to hear. The wind is 120 at 16, gusting to 25. runways 18 and 9 are active. In other words, the wind is from the southeast, strong and gusty, and I can choose a runway heading south, or one heading east. The 152's crosswind rating is only 12 knots. My logbook says I'm approved only for crosswind landings of less than 6 knots. This is a skill I need, and one I want to practice, but I don't like knowing what I'm about to do is beyond my experience and beyond the plane's good handling too.

I remember the training. Come in fast, only 20 percent flaps, maybe even only 10 percent. Add half the gust factor to your speed. Sideslip to keep your nose pointed down the runway, transition to the flare, and touch down out of that slip. And I remember the last thing Mark said to me before I left: "Don't be afraid to do a go-around."

I tell the tower I'll take runway 18. Sixty degrees of crosswind in a very light airplane, but that runway is wider than 9, and I figure I could use that width.

On final approach, I'm just not happy. My slip is bad, I'm not lined up, I imagine twisting the landing gear right off the airplane if I don't drive into the dirt, so ten feet off the ground I push in the throttle and tell the tower I'm going around.

Second try and I'm feeling much better. I'm lined up, and I have the feel of the transition nearly in my feet and hands when up goes the left wing again as I catch a gust, and suddenly I'm over the grass and dirt between the runway and a taxiway, my wheels skimming the top of the grass. In goes the throttle, and once more I tell the tower I'm going around, almost laughing to myself as I imagine their gasp, if anyone was watching, in those last few feet.

"You can use runway one three," the tower tells me.

One three! That's nearly dead into the wind! Why didn't they give me that in the first place, I wonder? But then another voice comes into my head. Why didn't I ask for it in the first place when I got here? I'm the one flying the airplane. There is no decision, not one, that isn't mine to make. If I planted this thing in the dirt, it would be my fault and no one else's.

The landing on one three is easy. And when I park the 152 at the Fargo Jet Center, turn it off and tie it down, get out and walk across the north ramp one more time, I understand again how much grace there is in this world. In front of me, in a few weeks, there will be the FAA written test, the oral exam, and the check ride. All of them will be difficult, and all of them will be exactly what every other pilot has passed. And when they are passed, there will be that little slip of paper in my wallet that says I am a pilot. But that slip of paper is only a permission. As I drive away from the airport, I want to call every pilot I know and tell them about today's landing. I know they would smile, and nod, and even though my story cannot compare with their own, each of them would remember their own first meetings with hard air.